# Why Does He Do That?

JUN '10

## THE KEY TO UNDERSTANDING WHY MEN DO WHAT THEY DO IN RELATIONSHIPS

## Gil Bryan

Outskirts Press, Inc.
Denver, Colorado

NOV    2009

Why Does He Do That?
The Key to Understanding Why Men Do What They Do In Relationships
All Rights Reserved
Copyright © 2007 Gil Bryan
V2.0

Outskirts Press
http://www.outskirtspress.com


ISBN-10: 1-59800-990-7
ISBN-13: 978-1-59800-990-3


Outskirts Press and the "OP" logo are trademarks belonging to
Outskirts Press, Inc.

Printed in the United States of America

NOV     2009

# Table of Contents

# Introduction
## Understanding the Process

*"Desire without knowledge is not good, and
to be overhasty is to sin and miss the mark."*
*–        Prov.19:2*

I saw her before she saw me. I noticed the look on her face and the pace at which she was walking, faster than normal and with a 'pinch of attitude'. Whatever was ailing her today, I knew I was going to be on the receiving end of it. Why? Because most of her problems stemmed from one of my 'kind' and, unfortunately for me, I was in the right place at the wrong time.

"That's it! That's it! I'm through dealing with you sorry men," my client, Pam, loudly protested to me, as though I personally did her wrong.

She continued, "Gil, I am so tired of dealing with your sorry brothers; they don't know what they want."

1

Pam, in true character, had arrived fifteen minutes before her scheduled appointment, so I was busy putting the final touches on the client in my chair. There were at least five or more customers in the reception area, waiting to get their hair or nails done by other technicians, but their presence didn't seem to affect her.

Besides being a punctual person, Pam was also very attractive, with a professional demeanor. She had a high-salary job and worked hard at it. Usually, after a long day at her office, she was quiet and reserved when she arrived to visit me. So I knew, by the way she entered the salon that day, she had a problem and, most likely, a serious one.

I tell you this about her to let you know that Pam wasn't a 'fly-by-night' young pup. She was an extremely strong, intelligent, and goal-oriented, thirty-something, professional woman. But as focused and successful as she was in her profession, she was just as helpless, frustrated, and confused, when it came to dealing with men on an intimate basis.

In an attempt to calm her down I asked her if she was all right? She answered in this unmistakable voice of desperation, "Yeah, I'm all right. It's your crazy brothers out there who are the problem. Gil, what's wrong with them?" This she asked, as though she really expected me to be the mouthpiece for all men.

Pam, like a lot of women I have encountered over the years, was frustrated with men. Everything she attempted to accomplish, when it came to dealing with the opposite sex, somehow or another seemed to go to pieces. She had always wanted to find a good man to settle down with. Someone, with whom she could share her dreams. Someone with whom she could 'let down her hair'.

She was tough at work, but behind her strength resided fears, insecurities, and unfulfilled desires. And all she wanted—no, all she needed—was to share that part of herself with someone special. However, no matter how hard she tried, that someone special seemed to always elude her.

Pam was truly sincere regarding her desire to be in a fulfilling relationship, but as honest as her intentions were, her actions were sincerely wrong. She had spent much of her adult life focusing on advancing her career and being self-sufficient, to the point where she wouldn't have to depend on a man. Now that she was ready to have a man 'fit into her life', she didn't have a clue on how to make 'it' work.

From the time she was a child, up until her adult life, her experience with men and relationships had been negative. She had seen her dad walk out, leaving her mom alone to raise her, her three brothers and little sister. She remembered the pain her mom endured and how hard she worked to support them. She witnessed the many disappointments and broken promises her mom experienced, 'waiting on a man' to save her.

She also heard the stories of her girlfriends, the lies they were told and the tears they shed, all because of some 'sorry man'.

Pam vowed she would never put herself in a similar situation, and would never depend on a man for anything. She was determined to be in a position where, if she did need something, she would get it herself.

Unfortunately, Pam is not the exception in today's society. In fact, she's the norm. There are a lot of women who have been disappointed, frustrated, brokenhearted, and confused, due to their lack of knowledge and misunderstanding of men and why they act the way they do and do the things they do.

And they do everything in their power to suppress their feelings for love. They become consumed in their careers. They go on shopping sprees and take trips they know they can't afford. Or they sleep around with men they have only known for a brief period of time. Never learning, but forever yearning. A yearning tucked deep down in their innermost being. A yearning desire that just won't go away -- the desire just to be loved.

But the same holds true for both sexes. Because there are a lot of men who are equally confused and hurt, with feelings of rejection, due to their lack of understanding and knowledge of women. And the sad thing about these men (and women), who have been wounded and hurt, is they go in and out of relationships, wounding and hurting others. They do the same thing to others that has been done to them. So the cycle continues.

But there is hope.

The key to that hope is through knowledge and understanding. For the most part, in today's society, we want something to work when we want it to, where we want it to, and how we want it to, without finding out why and how things are supposed to work in the first place. In other words, we seldom take the time to ask the 'manufacturer' of the thing why he created the thing in the first place. And what did He create this thing to do. And how we can get this thing that He created to work for our benefit.

And because we are a society of people that refuses to seek the knowledge and understanding of things, we stick labels on them. We are what I call a 'band-aid' society.

When we catch a cold, we call our selves 'sick' and we band-aid our sickness with medicine. We never stop and ask ourselves how or why we got sick in the first place. We just

As regards (i) and (ii), I think that the most reasonable thing to hold at this stage in the history of our subject is that propositional-attitude facts can't be identified with physical or topic-neutral facts, but that they do supervene on physical facts and that it is this supervenience that explains the counterfactual value of propositional-attitude because-statements. Ava stepped back because she saw that a car was speeding towards her, and this implies that, absent an extremely rare kind of overdetermination, she wouldn't have stepped back when she did if she hadn't seen that a car was speeding towards her. This is because if she hadn't seen that a car was speeding towards her, then she wouldn't have been in a certain neurophysiological state that was a cause of her stepping back. And this in turn is because her seeing that a car was speeding towards her supervened on a very large physical state, perhaps one stretching back into the past and taking in very complex relations to all sorts of distal things that included the neurophysiological state, and that neurophysiological state is a part of the large subvening state that wouldn't have obtained if the propositional-attitude state hadn't obtained. There remains the question about the modal sense in which propositional-attitude facts supervene on physical facts and the question about what accounts for this supervenience, but I have said what I'm able to say about those issues in 4.4.

As regards (iii), I hold three things. First, if propositional-attitudes require propositional-attitude causal laws, those laws will be *ceteris paribus* laws. Secondly, as I've argued elsewhere,[61] there is no explanatorily relevant sense in which there are any *ceteris paribus* laws: non-basic, or special-science, explanations don't use them and don't need them.[62] Thirdly, even if that weren't so, there wouldn't be relevant propositional-attitude *ceteris paribus* laws. As indicated above,[63] the best-candidate generalizations seem to be conceptual truths, not contingent causal laws. These, however, are big issues, and since I still believe what I've already published, I won't rehash them here.

As regards (iv), we could probably answer this pretty easily if we had a complete account of special-science explanations. My bet is that nothing here would give us reason to say that propositional-attitude explanations aren't causal explanations, especially since there isn't any good reason to think that causal-explanatory special-science notions must be related to underlying physical notions in any

---

[61] Schiffer (1991).    [62] Cf. Earman and Roberts (1999).

[63] 8.3; see also Schiffer (1991).

stronger sense than supervenience. For example, when we explain the decrease in the number of Mary's T4 cells in terms of her being infected with the HIV virion, that explanation isn't impugned by the fact that only some of the chemical properties definitive of HIV are essential to the decrease.[64] And while it is true that causal-explanatory propositional-attitude properties typically don't supervene on what is in the head, and thus can't be identified with any relevant 'causal powers' that are in the head, it is also plausible that many special-science explanatory notions are analogously 'wide'. For example, the property of being a gene doesn't supervene on the microstructural properties of DNA sequences, for, as Ron McClamrock points out, in order to be a gene something must contribute to the phenotype in ways that will typically depend on relations to other genetic materials and to the nature of the coding mechanisms that act on the DNA sequences. 'So the properties of a particular gene considered as that kind of DNA sequence are supervenient on its local microstructure, but its properties considered as that kind of *gene* are not.'[65] But these are very big issues and can't be dealt with here.

Finally, (v) has already been answered. The predictive value of propositional-attitude facts is absolutely crucial to their role in explanation. Propositional-attitude because-statements wouldn't have anything like the value they have for us if we didn't have the access we have to the propositional attitudes of others or if we couldn't use that access to predict what others will do. This predictive value falls under the evidentiary value of propositional-attitude facts generally, and this was explained in 8.2. Nothing other than pleonastic propositions could do their explanatory work as well as they do because nothing other than them could serve us as well in the systematic exploitation of head–world reliability correlations.

So we need pleonastic propositions, and in this book I've tried to give a theory both of what they are in themselves and of their place in nature, language, and thought.

---

[64] Cf. Schiffer (1991).  [65] McClamrock (1995: 29).

# REFERENCES

ADAMS, E. (1970), 'Subjunctive and Indicative Conditionals', *Foundations of Language*, 6: 89–94.

ALMOG, J., PERRY, J., and WETTSTEIN, H. (eds.) (1989), *Themes from Kaplan* (Oxford University Press).

ARMSTRONG, D. (1989), *Universals: An Opinionated Introduction* (Westview Press).

AUSTIN, J. L. (1962), *How to Do Things with Words* (Oxford University Press).

AYER, A. J. (1936), *Language, Truth and Logic* (Victor Gollancz).

BACH, K. (1997), 'Do Belief Reports Report Beliefs?', *Pacific Philosophical Quarterly*, 78: 215–41.

BARBER, A. (ed.) (2003), *Epistemology of Language* (Oxford University Press).

BARNETT, D. (forthcoming), 'Vagueness, Knowledge, and Rationality'.

BEALER, G. (2002), 'Modal Epistemology and the Rationalist Renaissance', in T. Gendler and J. Hawthorne (eds.), *Conceivability and Possibility* (Oxford University Press).

BEALL, J. (ed.) (forthcoming), *Liars and Heaps* (Oxford University Press).

BENACERRAF, P. (1965), 'What Numbers Could Not Be', *Philosophical Review*, 74: 47–73.

BENNETT, J. (2003), *A Textbook on Conditionals* (Oxford University Press).

BLACKBURN, S. (1984), *Spreading the Word: Groundings in the Philosophy of Language* (Oxford University Press).

BLOCK, N. (1980a), 'Troubles with Functionalism', in Block (1980b).

—— (1980b), *Readings in Philosophy of Psychology*, vol. i (Harvard University Press).

—— and STALNAKER, R. (1999), 'Conceptual Analysis, Dualism, and the Explanatory Gap', *Philosophical Review*, 108: 1–46.

BOGHOSSIAN, P. (1991), 'Naturalizing Content', in Loewer and Rey (1991).

—— and PEACOCKE, C. (eds.) (2000), *New Essays on the A Priori* (Oxford University Press).

BRADDON-MITCHELL, D., and JACKSON, F. (1996), *Philosophy of Mind and Cognition* (Blackwell).

BURGE, T. (1979), 'Individualism and the Mental', *Midwest Studies in Philosophy*, 4: 73–121.

—— (1980), 'The Content of Propositional Attitudes', Central Division APA talk, abstract published in *Noûs*, 14: 53–8.

—— (1982a), 'Other Bodies', in Woodfield (1982).

BURGE T. (1982b), 'Two Thought Experiments Reviewed', *Notre Dame Journal of Formal Logic*, 23: 284–93.

—— (1993), 'Content Preservation', *Philosophical Review*, 102: 457–88.

BYRNE, A. (forthcoming), 'Chalmers on Epistemic Content'.

—— and PRYOR, J. (forthcoming), 'Bad Intensions'.

CAMPBELL, J., O'ROURKE, M., and SHIER, D. (eds.) (2001), *Essays on Meaning and Truth* (Seven Bridges Press).

CHALMERS, D. (1996), *The Conscious Mind: In Search of a Fundamental Theory* (Oxford University Press).

—— (2002a), 'The Components of Content', in Chalmers (2002b).

—— (ed.) (2002b), *Philosophy of Mind: Classical and Contemporary Readings* (Oxford University Press).

—— (forthcoming), 'The Foundations of Two-Dimensional Semantics'.

—— and JACKSON, F. (2001), 'Conceptual Analysis and Reductive Explanation', *Philosophical Review*, 110: 315–61.

CHIHARA, C. (1979), 'The Semantic Paradoxes: A Diagnostic Investigation', *Philosophical Review*, 88: 590–618.

CHURCHLAND, PATRICIA (1986), *Neurophilosophy: Toward a Unified Science of the Mind/Brain* (MIT Press).

CHURCHLAND, PAUL (1981), 'Eliminative Materialism and Propositional Attitudes', *Journal of Philosophy*, 78: 67–89.

CODY, C. (1990), *Testimony: A Philosophical Study* (Oxford University Press).

COLE, P. (ed.) (1978), *Syntax and Pragmatics, ix: Pragmatics* (Academic Press).

CRIMMINS, M. (1992), *Talk About Beliefs* (MIT Press).

—— and PERRY, J. (1989), 'The Prince and the Phone Booth: Reporting Puzzling Beliefs', *Journal of Philosophy*, 86: 685–711.

DAVIDSON, D. (1980a), 'Actions, Reasons, and Causes', in Davidson (1980c).

—— (1980b), 'Mental Events', in Davidson (1980c).

—— (1980c), *Essays on Actions and Events* (Oxford University Press).

—— (1984a), 'On Saying That', in Davidson (1984c).

—— (1984b), 'Truth and Meaning', in Davidson (1984c).

—— (1984c), *Inquiries into Truth and Interpretation* (Oxford University Press).

—— (2001a), 'What is Present to the Mind', in Davidson (2001b).

—— (2001b), *Subjective, Intersubjective, Objective* (Oxford University Press).

DENNETT, D. (1988), 'Review of J. Fodor, *Psychosemantics*', *Journal of Philosophy*, 85: 384–9.

DEVITT, M., and STERELNY, K. (1987), *Language and Reality: An Introduction to the Philosophy of Language* (MIT Press).

DRETSKE, F. (1981), *Knowledge and the Flow of Information* (MIT Press).

—— (1988), *Explaining Behavior: Reasons in a World of Causes* (MIT Press).

—— (1990), 'Does Meaning Matter?', in Villanueva (1990).

DUMMETT, M. (1976), 'What is a Theory of Meaning? (II)', in Evans and McDowell (1976).

assume sickness is a part of being human. So we try and remedy our lack of knowledge for the reason we got sick in the first place with drugs that simply cover up the sickness instead of healing it.

When we get an 'upset stomach' or an ulcer, we band-aid our symptoms with Pepto-Bismol, Tagamet, or some other drug to ease our discomfort. We never take the time to understand our bodies or to learn the right kinds and combinations of food it requires.

When we see a child 'acting out', we label him a 'bad child', then we band-aid his actions by punishing him or filling him with drugs such as Ritalin. We never take the time to find out why that child is acting the way he is acting. And because we don't attempt to understand why things are the way they are, we become victims of our own ignorance.

*"My people are destroyed for lack of knowledge: because thou has rejected knowledge, I will also reject thee..." – Hos. 4:6*

Basically, in order to understand why things are the way they are, we must understand the process or the formula. Once you understand the formula, it doesn't matter what you plug into it, you are going to get the same results. For example, if you know that $a + b = c$, it doesn't matter what you plug into the formula, you still get the same results. And once you know the formula, you can always get it to work for you. For example, you could even change the order and say that $b - c = a$, or $a - c = b$.

Get the picture?

The same is true when dealing with the opposite sex. Once you understand why men act the way they do and do the things they do, dealing with a man becomes quite easy.

5

But why is it that we live in a society that doesn't seek to understand the formula or the process of things? I will tell you why. The one catch to understanding the formula or process of a thing or things is that you have to go back to the origin of a thing. Back to before it was created. When it was just a thought in the mind of the creator. Then, you must find out from the creator the purpose that he or she had for creating this thing. And the only way to understand how to deal with a man is to go back to his Creator. Which means you have to go back to God and find out what His plan and purpose was for creating man.

Unfortunately, in most of society, the last thing people want to believe is that there is a Supreme Being who has the solution to their problems. But once you understand there is a God who knows the answers to your problems, your eyes of understanding will be open, not only to seeing things for 'what' they are, but for 'why' they are.

As a woman, once you understand what God planned from the beginning for creating the man, you will never have another problem dealing with one. Because when it comes down to it, all men are made the same. What I mean is, all men operate based on the same formula. And once you learn the formula to what they run on, you won't have another problem dealing with men. You will never have to have a bad relationship, a bad marriage, a hard time dealing with men at work, or problems with your brothers, sons, or father. In fact, I urge you to not only learn these secrets, but also teach them to young girls and boys that you come in contact with so they can escape growing up with the same headaches, heartaches and frustrations you may have experienced.

**FIRST THINGS FIRST**

Before we get started down this fascinating road, there are a few things you must do. But, hold on. Don't think this is one of

6

those 'ooh it makes me feel good' books that you read and then go back to being the same person. You're going to have to do some work here. The only way to get real productivity out of your muscles is to work them, right? Well, the only way to get real productivity out of your brain muscle is to work it.

*The first thing I want you to do is to forget.*

That's right, forget about all those presuppositions you have concerning what you think a man should be and do. Clear your mind of all the data your girlfriends, your mama, your grandma, or even your Uncle Joe gave you, regarding what a man is supposed to be or do. Forget it! Most of the information we've collected over the years was received from well-meaning folks who didn't have a clue about what they were talking about.

How can you tell? Just look at their track records. How many people do you know, right now, who have the kind of relationship that you dream of having with your spouse? Not many, are there? I have asked hundreds of single men and women if they would like to have a relationship like their parents or married friends and, nine out of ten times, the answer is an astounding, "No!" In many cases, even if their parents have stayed together and raised them well, they still felt like their parents' relationship seemed to be missing something.

*The Second thing I want you to do is to take the time to love and understand you.*

No one else for right now, just concentrate on you. We spend so much time trying to love and understand others; we often lose sight of ourselves. And, we spend so much time giving to meet the needs of others; we end up starving our own needs. Then we wake up some fifty years later, looking in the mirror and asking the question, "Who is this person?"

***The third thing I want you to do is to practice sowing.***

That's right, I said sowing. If you don't learn the importance of sowing, you will never reap. Another way to say it is practice giving. Like I said, start with you first. Learn how to give to yourself and then practice on others. The key to getting out of, or into, any situation is in the sowing. So, the first thing you are going to need is a seed. But, if you want apples, you must sow apple seeds. And, if you want love, you must first sow love seeds.

I know a lot of people who are looking for love, but they are sowing the wrong type of seeds. If you want to receive love from a man you must sow 'love seeds' for him. But you are going to find out that what he sees as 'love seeds' is not what you might think. That is why learning what 'love seeds' are to a man may seem difficult to comprehend at first. And yes, it is going to go against what 95% of the people in the world are saying and doing. So you will be challenged. And you may even get a little discouraged. But, when you learn what 'love seeds' to plant in a man, in time, you will reap the fruit of your labor.

***Fourthly, take responsibility for where you are now.***

If your love life is not where you think it should be, don't blame anyone but yourself. Before I learned the principles that I am going to share with you in this book, I was saying the same things all the guys around me were saying. I was saying, "There just aren't any good women out there any more." And I was getting just what my words were saying, 'no good women'. Then one day, as I was reading the scriptures and meditating on the fact that I couldn't find a good woman, I read in Proverbs 26:2b "A curse causeless shall not come". For some reason that really struck a cord with me. I said, "What does that mean, Lord?" He prompted me to read it again. "A curse causeless shall not come." So I looked up the meaning of the word 'curse', which literally means bad thing, and the word 'causeless', which means 'on purpose' or 'through a cause'.

In other words, God was saying to me, if bad things are constantly coming my way, once I find the source or the cause of where they were coming from, I could stop the curse. More often than not, I found that most of the causes came from my own ignorance. So right then and there, I decided to erase all my excuses and take responsibility for the way my love life was unfolding.

Now, don't be like me. It took me almost four years to change, mainly because I still kept trying to do things my way. But, even though it took me a while to change, throughout the process, I was learning how not to be a victim, but to take charge of my life. Once I realized I was the one responsible for the direction in which my life was headed, and the only thing that was between my goals and me was a lack of knowledge and a lack of action, I refused to be the same.

***Lastly, I want you to act like it's already done in your favor.***

I want you to act like you have already achieved the type of relationship you desire. This is a powerful principle because your attitude determines how much, if any, fruit you get from sowing your seeds.

Let me give you an example. A newly married wife is at home waiting on her husband to arrive. He promised he would be home by seven o'clock so he could take her out to dinner; but it's now almost eight o'clock. She has two options which will determine how the rest of her night will go and which will set the tone for the rest of her marriage. Suppose she takes option one. While she sits there waiting on her husband to arrive, she becomes concerned that something terrible might have happened to him. She begins to imagine that he might have been in an accident. Then, through her relief and excitement to see him arrive home unharmed and safe, she runs outside, throws her arms around him, squeezes him tight, while kissing him all over and thanking God that He brought her husband home safe.

But suppose she takes option two. Instead of thinking about whether her husband is safe or not, she begins fostering thoughts of him being out with his pretty, new secretary. She surmises he is just like those 'no good men' she used to date before they got married. And, he must be a fool to think she is going to be sitting at home waiting on him, the way her mother used to sit at home waiting on her cheating father. Then, instead of being excited to see her newly wed husband, she develops a nasty and negative attitude. And as soon as he gets in the door, instead of lavishing him with love, she lashes out at him and gives him a 'piece of her mind'.

You see, every day we have the opportunity to choose blessings or cursings, life or death. The choice is ours. But let me warn you that any choice you make is going to have consequences, whether good or bad. Life is hard enough, so choose the good.

# Chapter 1
## The Source of Your Differences

**PERSONALITY TRAITS**

I know several books discuss different personality traits. You are not going to get that here. The problem I have with personality traits, regarding some people, is that once they discover what personality trait or traits they have, they use this information as an excuse for being, or staying, the same way. This is so, even if they know their ways are pushing away the people they claim to love.

One lady told me that she was part Melancholy (pessimistic), with a tendency to be negative, and part Phlegmatic (worrier) and couldn't help but be "set in her ways".

What kind of mess is that?

When you find a particular spot in your life that needs correcting; measure it up to the Word of God. If it doesn't come up to par with the Word, then change it. Do whatever you have to do, but don't let it control you. You control it. And, do what the Word of God tells you to do. In Philippians

11

2:5, the Word says: "Let this mind be in you, which was also in Christ Jesus..." The word "mind" here means "attitude". Do you think that Jesus had a negative attitude? Well, if He did, I don't think we would be here today.

### *You were not born that way*

Have you ever seen a person who is just mean and cranky? Tell me, how many times do you make it a point to be around them? Not many, do you? Not unless something is wrong with you, and you just like being around negative people and you like allowing them to steal your joy and bring you down.

Well, let me ask you, "Do you think that person was born that way?"

Of course they weren't. They have just let life, or situations in their life, dictate to them how they should react to certain situations. Consequently, they allow their actions to dictate their ways. Their ways take root within them and become a part of their personality.

This is not what God wants for us. God doesn't want us to become a victim of our ways and have them rule over us. Instead, He wants us to rule over them.

I have to admit I was once the same way. I would let my personality dictate how I should act. That was a horrible time for me, because one minute I was up and the next minute I was down. My emotions would change with the wind. It worked, at first, because it got me a lot of attention. People would come up to me and ask if "everything was alright." They would try to do things with the hope that I would be in a better mood. But that quickly wore off, especially with my close friends. In fact, even they stopped coming around me. They later told me that they got tired of trying to guess what mood I would be in that day. Jerks, so I thought.

### *The truth hurts*

I remember an incident that occurred when I was dating this particular young lady. *We were coming from church (seems like these things always happen after or before church) and we were going back and forth in a heated discussion. Before I knew what was happening, she slapped the dashboard with both hands and screamed at the top of her lungs, "Stop yelling at me!" Boy, did that shake me up, because I thought, right then and there, she was about to flip out. Then there was complete silence. I didn't say anything because I didn't want to see what would come next. After a few minutes, which seemed like an eternity, I asked her if she was all right. She finally spoke up and said, "Yes. I just hate it when you yell at me like that. Every time we get into a discussion, you are always yelling." I replied, "What do you mean, yelling? I wasn't yelling. I was just trying to get my point across." Then I started up again. I was so determined to defend myself that I kept going on. Then, I guess, my voice began to rise again, so she hit the dashboard of my car once more and screamed, "You're doing it again! Why can't you talk to me without getting upset and yelling?" I replied, with this puzzled look on my face, "I wasn't getting upset. I was just trying to explain myself. And I wasn't yelling." Finally, I shut up. I guess you can probably surmise that the rest of the day didn't fare too well.*

*I knew she was angry with me and I was definitely mad at her. I thought, "Who does she think she is, yelling at me and telling me I'm getting upset?" It's not my fault that she can't understand I'm just an emotional and expressive person." As soon as I got to her place, I quickly pulled up to her driveway, stopped the car, gave her the "you best get out look", and sped off towards my place. For the next few days, I didn't even call her. Well, maybe not a few days. Actually, for the next four or five hours, I didn't call her. When I finally did call, our conversation was very vague. I guess she was waiting for me to apologize and I was waiting for her to apologize. Even if she was right, I felt she could have expressed her feelings in a better way.*

Isn't it funny how the person, who is wrong, wants the other person or persons to correct him or her in a way they think is appropriate? And, the person in the wrong hates it when the other person(s) gives them a taste of their own medicine.

As the days went on, her comments really began to poke at me. So much so that, every time I went to pray, I couldn't, because all I could picture was her face and how adamant she was about me not yelling at her.

Now, let me tell you. I always thought that I was a good guy, so I figured the problem had to be hers. But the Lord wouldn't let me rest with that. I began to do the hardest thing in the world. During the next few weeks I started to judge myself. Even though I knew she had faults of her own, I was determined to look only at me and analyze my faults.

As I did, I started remembering the times when other people had told me about my big mouth and my hot emotions. I recalled the times when I almost got into school fights, blurting out something to make the kid, I was talking to, mad. (I felt that it was important to have a quick tongue. Besides, I enjoyed it when all the other kids would laugh at my clever remarks.)

Several weeks later, my ex and I made up, so, I decided to bring her home with me for Thanksgiving. At the dinner table sat my youngest sister, my mom, my brother and his girlfriend, my other sister and her fiancé, and me and my ex. As I sat there, I observed how my family was acting. We were all telling jokes, laughing, and yelling at one another. It seemed as if I was having an out-of-body experience. I thought, "Who are these people?" I was seeing my family and myself in a different light. My ex, on the other hand, was sitting on the end of the table next to me, as quiet as a mouse and in her own world. I tapped her and said, "See, this is where I get my loudness. It's not my fault."

Don't get me wrong. I'm not saying anything was wrong with my family being loud, laughing, and having a good time. I just never took the time to see things from another person's point of view. From that time on, after that rude awakening, I committed myself to change.

From then on, every time I was talking to or with someone, I would try to catch myself when I thought I was getting too emotional, or too loud, or too upset. I didn't just say, "This is my personality and you are going to have to deal with it." I wanted to, in a sense, judge myself. Consequently, by first judging myself, it helped me to better understand me and understand why God created me to be the way I am. You see, I like motivating and teaching people. That's what I do. God has gifted me with great passion for certain things. But if my gift is not guided in the right direction, it can be a curse instead of a blessing.

Not only did I change how I spoke with people, but I also changed the way I perceived things. From then on, I made an effort, whenever I was conversing with someone, to try and see things from their point of view.

That is why I say I don't like it when people use personality traits as a crutch. I do think it is wise, when dealing with people, to get an understanding of your personality, first, and then get an understanding of their personality. But don't let your personality dictate who and what you are and how you should act. Nor should you let a person's personality prevent you from seeing who they really are and their true nature.

When God speaks to us, He is not concerned about our personality traits. Imagine telling God, "I can't be in a good mood today, God, because it is not in my personality." When God speaks to us, He speaks to that inward being that is made in His image and His likeness. And that being which dwells in us, and is made in God's image, never has a bad day.

**THE 3 LOVE PRINCIPLES**

Now the real question is, "Why do men do some seemingly stupid stuff?" O.K., maybe not seemingly stupid, maybe the stuff is stupid. But, why is this so? Let's first analyze what we think is stupid versus what God says is good. God is the one who created the man, so, He had to know that what He was putting in the man had to be good for the woman.

Before we go any further, there are some things you must understand about God. The first thing is, God is Love. And Love has three rules or principles it must abide by.

### *Love Principle #1 states "For love to exist, love must give"*

Love does not have a choice in this matter. If Love is to exist, it must give; it is propelled to give. In other words, if that special someone is not giving or showing you love, but instead they are stealing your joy, your peace of mind, your happiness, and your fun, then wipe your tears and move on. 'Cuz it ain't love.'

Love is the reason God was motivated to create Man, spirit-man, that is. See, we all know God is all-powerful, all knowing, and ever-present. But one thing we seem to forget is that God is Love. God is not just a part of Love. God is Love. Now there is a funny thing about Love. See, you can be all-powerful, all knowing, and ever-present, all by yourself, but one thing you cannot be, by yourself, is Love.

But if God is the only God, and there is none like Him, no one as powerful as Him, to whom is He going to give His love to or share His love with? Because God searched His whole self, the whole entire universe, the galaxies, the eons and eons of time and space that is within Him, and found no one that could appreciate his gift of love. Which brings us to principle number two.

***Love Principle #2 states that "The Giver of Love and the Receiver of Love must be made up of the same components"***

For love to come full circle or be complete, the one who gives love and the one who receives love must be just alike or made up of the same components.

Which means, no matter how much affection you have for your pet, it isn't true or Godly love because your pet isn't like you. Your pet does not have God's Spirit within and therefore is not made up of the same components that you are made up of.

But, wait a minute. We just found out there was no one like God. So, how is God going to get another 'Him' to give love to, since another 'Him' does not exist?

Answer: God has to take out a part of Himself in order to create another 'self'.

Now let's go to scripture and prove this. We know that, in the beginning, God created the heavens and the earth and all the wonderful creatures. But before God made all these things, he created this being called spirit-man. In Ephesians 1:4 Paul writes that we were "...chosen in him before the foundation of the world." In essence, before God *made* all the other things, such as the sun, the moon, the stars, the earth, etc., He had already *created* spirit-man (us).

17

In other words, God decided to have children. But, like the Good Father that He is, before making His children, He wisely put in place everything they would need. And, not only did He want to make sure His children's needs were provided for, He also wanted them to always think and act like Him; so He also provided them with food, seed (to make more food), servants (angels), money (gold and silver), and anything else they would need.

In Ephesians, Paul was talking about our spirit bodies because, at this point, the dirt or soil part of us called the 'humus' was not yet made.

Where do you think the word human came from? The word human comes from two words, which are 'humus' and 'man'. Our ancestors learned, a long time ago, that man is made up of two distinct parts. One is dirt or soil, which is called humus. This is the part of us that is seen with the natural eye. And the other is man, which is called spirit. This is the part of us that is seen with the spiritual eye. So, I can't just call you a 'humus' being. That would be half true. I must call you a 'humus-man' being or 'human' being, in order to tell the whole truth.

So, God had to do something. God said, "I Am God and I Am Love. I must find someone to love."

So God said to Himself, "Let me make one like me to love." So Bam! God creates another him by pulling a piece of him out of Himself. The scriptures say in Gen 2:27 "...God created man in is own image, in the image of God created He him..." In other words, this one is going to be exactly like Me in character and makeup.

Now, here was this creature God had just created, who now has the same likeness and image of God. So, God decides to give this creature, whom He just created, a gift in order to show his love. Which brings us to Principle #3.

*Love Principle #3 states that It's the Receiver of Love who determines what Love is and not the Giver of Love*

In other words, you shouldn't just give someone a gift and expect him or her to love the gift and love you for giving it. You must first find out how the person, whom you want to give your gift of love to, interprets love, and then make every effort to give them what they want. We will discuss more about this topic later.

So, let's continue. After God created this being He could Love, called spirit-man, He decides to give this man a gift called earth. Since man (spirit) came from God, God must know what he needs for love.

How? Because God is not only the receiver of love in this case, He is also the giver of love. It is He who dwells in man.

That is why, if you want to know what a man or woman needs in regards to love, all you have to do is ask God. Because, no matter how mean or nasty one might be on the outside, there is a spirit or God-like nature on the inside.

That is also why God never expects anything less from us. In fact, He expects man (spirit-man, that is) to be like Him. God says, in 1 Peter 1:16, for us to 'be Holy, for I AM Holy'. Now, how could a Perfect and Holy God expect man to be Holy? Because God knows Who dwells on our inside... a part of Him.

So, God gives this spirit-man a gift called earth. And God says to this man, 'Be like me and dominate and subdue this earth. But you have to watch me, and listen to me, and do what I do, and you won't have any problems.'

Now everything is going great. The man is excited about getting this big gift from God, called earth. But uh-oh, the man soon realizes something. He can't get a hold of his gift. So the man says to God, "I am spirit and the earth is made out of dirt. How can I affect the earth?" So God says, "Calm down. Calm down. I know exactly what you need. You need a dirt suit. Because the only way for you to be able to affect the earth is to become a part of it." So God scoops up some of the dirt from the earth and sculpts it and frames it. Then He puts the spirit-man, whom he just created, in this pile of dirt. That is why in Gen. 2:7, it states, "God formed man out of the dust of the ground and breathed into his nostrils the breath or spirit of life, and the man, or Adam, became a living soul."

Note: Why do you think the spirit-man is so important to God? The spirit is the part of us that came from God and therefore the spirit-man will never die. The word death in the bible does not exactly mean to exist no more. A better meaning of the word death is 'to be separated from your source of survival.' For example, fish need water to live. If you take the fish out of the water, and therefore separate it from its source of survival, it will eventually die. In relationship to the man, the bible talks about two kinds of death. The first death is to be separated from the body or the dirt house. Another kind of death, which is the second death, is to be separated or cut off from God.

So now, at this point, everybody is happy. God is happy because He now has man to love. Man is happy because he has God to love. And man can enjoy the gift that God just gave him. But uh-oh! While man was busy unwrapping his gift and playing with his new toys, God noticed something. Then God spoke and said, "It is not good for man to be alone...," or 'all-one'.

This man, Adam, is made up of the same material that God is made up of, Spirit. But, he is also made up of the earth or dirt. This presents a problem for Adam. Remember Principle #2 of Love states, 'For love to be complete the receiver and the giver have to be just alike.' So, God and Adam can exchange or

20

reciprocate love through their Spirit relationship. But Adam is also made up of dirt; he now needs someone to relate to that dirt or earthly part of him.

So God says to Adam, you can't love the animals, even though they are made of the earth (dirt), because animals are not like you. They have no "spirit". There is no scripture in the bible that records any animal as having God's Spirit. So God observed and concluded, "It is not good (sufficient, satisfactory) that the man should be alone (or all-one); I will make him a help-meet suitable for him." Gen. 2:18 -AMP

Adam now was at the same place God was before God created spirit-man. Remember that before God created spirit-man, there was no one like God to love. So God had to take a piece of Him to create a mini Him. A being just like Him.

So God does the same thing to Adam. God takes a piece of Adam and makes another being just like Adam. In Gen. 2:22 it states, "And the rib or part of his side which the Lord God had taken from the man, He built up and made into a woman..."
Note: The word for 'rib' here is the Hebrew word tselah (sel `a). It is where we get our modern word cell.

So, by taking a rib or cell from Adam, God made a being that is just like Adam. But this new being came from two sources. First, she came from God and, therefore, is made up of God's Spirit (remember when God first created spirit-man both the male and the female were in Adam); but she also came from Adam's rib or flesh. So the woman can receive 'spiritual' love from God and earthly or fleshly 'love' from Adam. That is why it was Adam, who saw, concluded, and said about this being that God just made for him that "This is now bone of my bone and flesh of my flesh, so she shall be called Man." Oops! Can't call her Man because she has a womb and she is my receiver. Therefore, she shall be called receiver-man or 'wombed-man' (woman).

# Chapter 2

## Why He Is The Way He Is

*When You Understand Why a Man Is*
*The Way He Is, You Can Get His Stuff!*

The way a man is is based on his nature. If you understand the nature of a man, and use it to your benefit, you can get him and everything that comes with him... his money, his time, his love, his car, etc. Webster defines nature as 'the inherent characteristics or inherent tendencies of a thing.' For example, the nature of water is wet. When you get the water you get the wet.

But it is not just enough to understand the man's nature; as a woman, you must understand your nature. You must understand why you were created and why you are compelled to do the things you do. For example, as a woman you must realize that you are going to show emotions and that it's o.k. The last thing you want is to try and not show emotions. On the other hand, you don't want your emotions to control you. What you want to do is learn and understand why you are the way you are. Once you understand your nature, and therefore the nature of all women, you can begin understanding how your nature works in conjunction with the man's nature. Then you can live the godly life that God desires you to live. This will not only make you a male magnet, it will prevent you from having to go through life with a lot of heartaches and frustration dealing with men, or people in general for that matter.

**WHAT GOD CREATED THE MAN TO DO**

A man's nature or inherent characteristics are not based on what either you or I think it should be. They are based on what he was created to do.

There are three main things that the man was created to do. I am talking about what God had originally planned when he created the man.

The first thing God created the man to do is to lead; the second is to cultivate; and the third is to guard and protect.

When God decided to create mankind, God wanted a family that was to be just like Him. Therefore, God knew these creatures would want to rule, dominate, and be in control. They were created to rule together but in different roles. God never did command the man to dominate or to control the woman, or the woman to dominate or control the man. God wanted the man and the woman to unite as one in marriage and, through this combining of different strengths, the man and the woman were to reign and rule together over the earth. This is why Paul writes that marriage is such a great mystery. There is power in the unity of holy matrimony.

Husbands and wives have been fighting with each other for years, not realizing there is strength in unity. All the while, the one they were commanded to keep under control (satan) is kicking back, having a ball. Well, why shouldn't he be living it up? He doesn't have anything to worry about, because the ones that can stop him are too busy fighting each other.

Ever wonder where the term divorce comes from? Whenever there are two visions in the same house you have a 'di' vision or division. The prefix, 'di' means two. Whenever there is a division or two separate visions, it will lead to a 'di' force'. 'Di', which means two, and 'force' or 'vorce', which means power. Hence, a divorce is the separating of two powers. When there is a separation of powers, the one strong power now becomes two weaker powers. So goes the saying, "A house divided against itself shall fall."

That is why it is imperative that you realize, first of all, that it is not your mate who is the problem. Behind the scenes is satan. His job is to keep you ignorant of God's purpose for one another. Because, when you don't know and understand the purpose of a thing, you can't help but to misuse and abuse it.

Remember, God is a God of purpose. So, whenever God does something, He does it with a purpose in mind. God doesn't make any mistakes. If God created something, no matter what your opinion is concerning it, God sees the good in it, because He knows and understands why He created it in the first place.

**TO LEAD**

Position determines function. The man was created first; therefore, he was put in the leadership position. Because God placed the man in the leadership position, God had to supply him with everything he needed to carry out the leadership role.

### *Why Does He Always Want To Be In Control?*

I have a client named Angie who is a very attractive young lady in her mid-twenties. She has an excellent job at an Internet support company where she is the manager of several employees. Her boyfriend Allan works for the same company in a lesser-paying job. They both attend the same church and are looking forward to getting married soon. The problem they are having is that, when they are together, Angie feels Allan always has to play the power game. She complains that Allan is too controlling and is always trying to tell her what to do. She says that no man has ever told her what to do and she doesn't expect it to start now. Not to mention, if he is like this now, she feels things will only get worse after they get married.

Unfortunately, most men don't know how to be a good godly leader, so they feel that being controlling is the same as being in control. But remember, every man has within him the potential to be a leader, no matter what state he is in now. Because of this innate quality in him to lead, he is going to feel that he needs to always be in control.

Because most men weren't taught how to be a good leader, he may feel intimidated by a woman who is smart and aggressive. But a smart woman can diffuse this part of her man by simply giving him 'space'. In other words, when a person acts a certain way, don't put up your dukes and fight with them. Just lovingly and respectfully let them know that you don't appreciate the way they are treating you. And if the action persists, go your way and leave them be.

*For example, Angie can say to Allan, "Allan, I appreciate your willingness to be in charge, but it will make me feel more appreciative if you include me in your decision-making process. When you don't include me, it makes me feel like you don't love me."*

*Whoa! Won't that get Allan's attention? But Angie has to be strong. If Allan continues to act the same way, no matter how much she loves him, she is going to have to pull away and give him the space he needs to decide if their relationship is important enough for him to change. If she continues to stay in the relationship and doesn't see any signs of change, then she is silently telling Allan that she really didn't mean what she said and, in fact, she is condoning the way he treats her.*

### A MAN DOESN'T QUALIFY TO BE THE 'HEAD' OF HIS HOUSE

What too many men are trying to do is qualify themselves to be the head of their household or relationship, so they are trying to force their way into a position that already belongs to them.

They must realize that in God's eyes, they are the 'head' or leader. So, the responsibility of leading is going to be on them. And this responsibility has nothing to do with how smart a man is, how much money a man makes, his age, or anything else for that matter. He is the Head. Period.

See, in the above example, Allan knows that Angie has a higher position than he does in the company and that she makes more money than he does. So, by him acting as if he "knows everything" and by him being controlling, he is really showing his insecurity.

Now, I think it's all right for Angie to encourage Allan to take his rightful place as 'head' of their relationship and to remind him of who he is in God's eyes, every now and then, but if she has to keep reminding him of who he is, all the time, then it may be in her best interest to let him go so he can 'find' himself.

### QUALITIES OF A LEADER

A leader must have vision. In other words, a leader must have goals and desires for himself and for his family. "Where there is no vision the people perish." -Prov. 29:18. A lot of problems occur in relationships because many men don't know where they are going. And too many women jump on board a ship that isn't going anywhere. That is why, in the old bible days, a man would have to bring a dowry to the father. A dowry was a specified amount of money, cows, sheep, land, etc., that a man brought to show that he had something going for him (not just a good idea), and to express his sincere desire to marry this man's daughter. In other words, you had to 'put up or shut up'.

Unfortunately, in our society today, people spend more time qualifying the type of vehicle they want to buy, than they do qualifying a perspective mate. As a woman, it's imperative that you first find out what a man's vision for his life is. Then, determine if you are willing to do what is needed to support his vision. Now, if his vision does not include you, or if his vision is going to take you some place you don't want to go, that should be a good hint for you to keep moving. Because what he sees is what he is going to produce.

I know of a particular couple that is having problems in their marriage because the wife doesn't want any children and the husband does. All this could have been solved if they had received the proper counseling and discussed their future plans, before they got emotionally involved.

Now ladies, if he doesn't have a vision, the worst thing you can do to a man is to try and give him a vision. It won't work! Because you are now out of position. Instead of him leading you, you are trying to lead him. Remember, it is the head that has to have the vision. And, besides, you don't want that position, because God didn't create you to be in that position. Now I did not say that God did not create you to lead. In fact, many women in today's society happen to be better leaders than most men. But in a marriage relationship, the 'Head' role is not the position God created you to be in. In the marriage relationship, God created you to help. Your job is to help the man to fulfill the vision that God has placed in his heart. We

28

will talk more about that in Chapter 3.

## WHY IS HE ALWAYS LOOKING AT OTHER WOMEN WHEN WE GO OUT?

*For every truth in the spiritual realm there
is a parallel truth in the physical or natural realm.*

As stated earlier, in order for a man to lead, he must have a vision. His vision guides his pathway and motivates him in the direction he needs to go. Without a vision or spiritual eyes, he won't go anywhere. But just as he is motivated and stimulated by his vision or spiritual eyes in the spiritual realm, he is going to be motivated and stimulated by what he sees in the physical realm.

So when a young lady with a short, tight dress passes by your man, he may have a tendency to look and may look hard. But don't get mad, throw a fit, or get an attitude at him for looking, or get mad at the woman for wearing the outfit. Just acknowledge the outfit the woman has on and remind him not to stare too hard, because staring is not the right thing to do in the presence of a lady, you.

## WHY CAN'T HE MAKE A DECISION?

Some men are too controlling and some men don't want any control. So they don't make any decisions, because they don't want to be responsible if things go wrong.

I was talking to a client of mine a while back and something about her was just not clicking for me. I kept wondering how this young, attractive lady, with a good-paying job, her own house, a nice sports utility vehicle, and a supposedly great boyfriend, who was doing equally as well, could not be married yet. She and her boyfriend had been dating for over two years and she claimed they were ready to get married. I determined they either didn't really want to get married, though she swore they did, or something else was amiss.

Well, one day I just couldn't take it any more. So I asked her, "Sherrie, you mean to tell me you have all this going for you, and you say you want to get married, but you're no closer to getting married now than when I first met you six months ago." I continued, "Something doesn't seem right." Do you know what she did? She swung around in my chair and said "You are so right, Gil! My boyfriend is a momma's boy! He's so weak; I just can't take it! He won't make any decisions. I have to make them all by myself!"

Boy, that really caught me off guard. Not particularly what she said, but how adamant she was about what she said. But, she is not alone. There are plenty of women out there who are experiencing this same thing. There are so many men who are so weak that women feel like they have to stand up and take the man's position. But I warn you – no, I beg you – not to take that weight upon yourself, because that is not what you want. In fact, it will do you well to leave him right where he is and focus your attention elsewhere. Whenever your man depends on you to make the decisions, no matter how much you want to, don't. You don't want to be put in the position of being the one in the 'head' or leadership role. You don't want that responsibility. I'm not saying that you can't make decisions; all I am saying is that you don't want to go there. In the long run, it will weaken you both.

Years ago in college a few friends of mine, Chrystal and Jesse, got married. They looked like the perfect couple. Jesse was tall, strong, and handsome and Chrystal was just…fine. Matter of fact, they looked like they just stepped out of *Jet Magazine*. They dated the entire time throughout college, and right after they graduated – or actually, when she graduated – they got married. Jesse never finished college.

Boy, were they doing great, until one day when Chrystal's job downsized.

Right after she was downsized, their marriage went to pieces. Why? According to Chrystal, Jesse wasn't pulling his weight and now that she didn't have a job, she couldn't afford to carry the household expenses and him too. But wait a minute. They have been together for ten years, and she has always carried Jesse.

In other words, since she was making the lion's share of the money, she was the one who made most of the decisions: where they lived, the kind of house they would live in, where Jesse worked, what car was best for them. And now, because she was without a job, she wanted Jesse to step up to the plate and take his rightful position as head of their household. But Jesse wasn't up to the task. Having always followed Chrystal's lead and suddenly being catapulted into this role as the leader or head of the household, he couldn't handle it.

What a lot of women fail to realize is that neither money, nor education, nor job rank determines your role. The man is the head by God's decree, not by whether you or I think he should be.

**WHY CAN'T HE BE MORE RESPONSIBLE WITH THE FINANCES?**

This is especially true in the financial area. I know of several relationships where the wife is the one responsible for the finances. In my house, for many years, my wife was responsible for doing the finances.

Let me tell you why that is not good. But, before I start, let me say that I am not saying women can't do the finances. Because in many cases, due to a woman's good memory and need for security, she may be better at keeping the finances in order than her man. She is going to make sure the bills are paid and household needs are taken care of. But the problem arises when the woman is put in the position of being *responsible* for the finances to a point where the man doesn't know where they stand financially.

All he does is go out and spend money like there is no tomorrow. Then, when he goes to her and tells her he wants more money so he can buy himself a new set of golf clubs, and she says, "We can't afford it," he wants to get angry with her. He starts to moan and complain that he is working all the time but can't spend a little bit of his hard-earned money.

The weight of having to tell her husband and/or her children that they can't buy something, especially when there is a full-grown man in the house, puts undue stress on the woman.

Besides, it's the man whom God called to be the provider. But to provide, he must have a 'pro' for his vision. The prefix 'pro' means of support. But how can a man have means for support, or rather provision for his vision, if he doesn't know where he stands financially. This doesn't mean that the man has to make more money than the woman. It just means that they have to be in agreement with the provision (the finances) for the vision to come to pass. To come to an agreement they both have to know and understand their financial condition.

**A LEADER MUST BE ABLE TO STAY FOCUSED**

Ever notice when a man is watching T.V. how he hates being distracted. Or when he is in a conversation, he can only focus on one person speaking at a time - unlike women, who can have two or three conversations going on at the same time. This is because the man was created with the responsibility of leading and a leader must be able to be focused.

That is why it's dangerous when a man tells a woman he is working on one project this week and then tells her he is working on another project the next week, when he hasn't finished the first one.

The better he can be at staying focused, the less emotional ups and downs the woman has to go through. When a man tells a woman that he is going to do something, it becomes part of her. It goes straight down into her womb and she begins to conceive it. And what makes many women so frustrated is, just when they are about to give birth to the idea or dream the man gave her, he goes and changes his mind and comes up with another so-called great idea. And here she is stuck with this stillborn baby in her womb.

*"When you go against your nature, you will suffer"*

I remember when I used to work in this particular salon. Every day when I left the salon, I would leave with a severe headache. At this time, I was still young in the Lord, so I figured every time something bad happened to me; it had to be satan's fault. I would go in speaking the Word and I would leave speaking the Word, but I would still leave with the worst headache in the world.

One day, I decided that instead of trying to fight this battle on my own I would wise up and go to the Lord about it. Now mind you, I was still coming into the knowledge of the differences between men and women, so, I had no clue of what was going on. Well, anyway, when I went to pray, the Lord just sort of whispered in my spirit for me "to be quiet."

Be quiet? What did He mean by that? I was so puzzled by what I thought the Lord had said to me that the next day that I went into work, I barely said a word. I was listening and waiting for further instructions from the Lord.

Well, lo and behold, as I started to listen to what was going on around me, my eyes were opened. For the first time, I realized where my problem was coming from. Though not an unusual situation, I was the only man in that beauty salon, working with three women. I had a woman on the left side of me, another on my right, and one straight across from me. And, all three were carrying on conversations at the same time-- with their clients, with my clients, and with each other. In the middle of all this, I was trying to be like them and trying to give each one of them my attention. The strain of trying to focus on what each person was saying was causing my brain to split in two.

My first thought was how thoughtless, how inconsiderate and rude these women were. They weren't even listening to one another. They were all talking over each other and cutting each other off. Then I realized something. To them, they weren't being rude or inconsiderate. They, as women, have the ability to have more conversations going on at once and this is different from me.

*Lack of knowledge doesn't cancel a thing; it*
*just causes it to be used for the wrong purpose.*

Let's suppose a man doesn't know that the reason he has been given the ability to stay focused on one thing at a time is so he can accomplish the vision God has for him. He is still going to use this ability, but it won't be directed in the way God had intended when God created the man. Instead of the man being focused on completing his vision, he will be focused on watching T.V., playing games, or taking care of his ride. There are many men who are focusing their attention on temporary things and denying their wives and children the attention that they crave.

**TO TEACH AND CULTIVATE**

*Why does he always want to tell me what to do?*

There is at least one particular topic that every man feels he knows everything there is to know about it, and he wants to let you know he knows it, too. No matter how wrong he may be. And, if you spend most of your time trying to get him to admit that he is wrong, then you are wasting your time.

Men hate admitting they are wrong or that they don't know something. This is because God put in every man the desire to teach or cultivate those whom he feels are under his care. In Gen. 2:15 it states that "...the Lord God took the man, and put him into the Garden of Eden to dress it..."-KJV. The word dress means to cultivate. Cultivate means to prune, till, to put in the right ingredients and also to teach.

You could be driving somewhere with a man and, though he knows he is lost, he won't stop and ask for directions.

But, though he won't ask for directions, he will want to give you directions. He wants to tell you how to dress, what friends to hang around, or how to jump out of a plane (even though he has never done it himself). Whatever the subject is, he wants to make you believe that he knows everything there is to know about it.

Now, this very nature of a man, most women fight against. They say, "My father didn't tell me what to do. And no man is going to start telling me what to do." Though she may not realize it, this attitude she has is cutting at his very nature and will eventually push him further and further away from her.

**TO GUARD AND PROTECT**

The third thing God created the man to do was to guard and

35

protect. In Gen. 2:15, it continues "...the Lord God put the man in the garden to dress it and keep it." To keep is the Hebrew word which means to guard and protect. This need that a man has to protect, or rather, 'look after' what he considers his, the world calls the ego.

*This ego is so sensitive that when a man feels like it is being threatened, he will do whatever it takes to protect it.*

You can identify a man's need to protect by watching the little things he does. For example, when you go to a restaurant with a man, he will tend to sit facing the entrance or exits. Whenever he goes into an unfamiliar area, he is always concerned about what is going on around him. And, it may take him awhile to get comfortable in a new environment.

If you stay out too long shopping, he will drill you for not being more responsible. If you wear an outfit that he thinks is too short on you, especially when he's not around you, he may not want you to wear it. Or he may want you to wear it only when you are out with him.

I had a client who recognized that she had threatened her fiancé's ego when she told him she didn't need his help. She told me she was getting out the ladder to change the light bulb, like she always did. But this time, her fiancé, who lived out-of-state, was there, and, when he realized what she was doing, he said to her, "Honey let me get that for you." Because she didn't know any better at the time, she started thinking to her self, "Who does he think I am? I am not a helpless little girl who can't do anything. I don't need his help. I've been taking care of myself since way before he came along. Who does he think changes the light bulb when he's not here?" So she said to him with as much restraint and politeness as she could muster up, "Oh, that's all right, I can do it myself."

Right after that incident occurred, it seemed like he got a little attitude with her, so she got an attitude with him. Now they weren't even talking to each other, and neither one of them realized what had happened. Until our conversation, she was seeing things from her point of view. Only thing she was seeing was, that if he is acting like that now, he would only get worse after they were married. So, she concluded by telling me she felt they were just not meant for each other.

She had no clue that her attitude of independence was interpreted by him as an "I-really-don't-need-you" attitude and was, therefore, pushing him away from doing what he felt he was called to do. Which is to look after her.

### WHY IS HE SO COMPETITIVE?

As we mentioned earlier, when God created the man, he put in him the desire to lead. This, compounded with his desire to guard and protect, causes the man to be very competitive.

Because of this competitive nature in him, he will say things like, "let's bet," or, "I bet you can't do that!" This is why many men get into sports. But it doesn't have to be sports. It can be computers, video games, or just eating. Whatever it is he enjoys doing, he is going to want to compete at it. Whenever you see a man who has lost his desire to compete, you have a crushed man. Without a desire to compete, a man has nothing to motivate him to accomplish the goals and visions God has for his life.

This desire to compete is also evident in young boys. I know every time I'm around my nephews, they are wanting to race me, or play against me in basketball, or whatever they think they can beat me in.

Now, this very nature in men (and boys) can be very frustrating to women. I remember riding in the car with my mom, while my nephew (he was about eight years old at the time) was huffing and puffing in the back seat. Then he said to his grand mom (my mom), "Grandma, you are letting everybody pass you!" My mom, not understanding this competitive nature, felt like he was criticizing her driving. So, she told him to sit back and be quiet because, "I was driving before you were born!"

He wasn't trying to be critical. He wasn't even concerned about how well she could drive. In fact, his concern was more about quantity than about quality. His competitive nature was screaming, "All the cars are beating us!" and "I don't want to be last!"

*A man's competitive nature, combined with his nature to guard and protect, will cause a man to die for something he believes in.*

There are young men in gangs who are willing to put their lives on the line, or even take another person's life, just to guard and protect a particular color or his turf (which is usually a particular piece of property that doesn't even belong to him).

This nature is going to be expressed in a man – whether it's for good or for bad. But, God wants him to use this nature for good. Instead of a man being so ready and willing to die to protect a particular plot of land or color, He wants him to use that same nature to guard and protect his family. Same nature. Same energy. But now directed in the right way.

Satan knows about this competitive nature that is in the man. So, he wants to make sure he keeps the man blinded as to who he really is and what he was called to do, so he can use man's own strength to destroy himself.

Believe me, you want a man who is competitive. And the more

competitive he is, the better it is for you.

Why?

Let's assume your man is not treating you the way you want him to treat you. You should already know by now that I am talking about a real man. And a real man is not physically abusive, verbally abusive. Nor is he a liar, cheat, or drug addict. If he is in not in any of these categories, or categories like these, watch what happens when you start to treat him with respect. When you start considering him before you decide to do something. When you fix him his favorite meal, even after he forgot to get you a birthday gift. Or, when you don't fuss and nag him when he loses his job again.

Once you have decided to "be good" to him, no matter what he does or says, his competitive nature is going to rise up in him and say, "I'm not going to let her outdo me." And, before you know it, those things you thought he wouldn't do for you, he is going to be compelled to do, without you having to say a word.

Remember, real men hate losing, no matter what the situation. So be smart and use this valuable tool wisely.

# Chapter 3
## Why She Is The Way She Is

Just as there are three primary things God created the man to do, there are also three primary things God created the woman to do. The first thing God created the woman to do is to be 'good' for the man, the second is to be 'a helper' for the man, and the third is to be 'fit' or 'suitable' for the man.

### *To be Good for the Man*

God said, "It is *not* good that man should be alone…" -Genesis 2:18a. The first thing God created the woman to be is 'good' for the man. The word 'good' actually is translated 'perfect' or the 'best thing' for the man. With God, there is either good or bad. Not this 'kind of bad' stuff or this 'kind of evil' stuff. Either you are perfect (good) or you are imperfect (evil). In Matt. 7:11 Jesus says, "that if you then, being evil (imperfect), know how to give good gifts unto your children, how much more shall your Father which is in heaven give good things to them that ask Him?" -KJV. God is not saying here that you are the 'devil' kind of evil. He is saying that you are in the flesh and, therefore, under sin, so you can't be good (perfect). But

41

you can do good deeds and give good gifts.

So, as a woman you must decide whether or not you are willing and prepared to be good for your man. Being good for him includes, but does not limit, the fact that once you decide to accept him and, therefore, accept his 'vision', the vision he has becomes both of yours. Once the vision becomes both of yours, from that point on, you commit to doing everything in your power to help the vision come to pass.

Being good for him may mean that you do your best to have a positive and cheerful attitude, even if your man isn't acting the way you think he should act. A negative attitude is only going to push him farther away from you.

Being good for him may mean he might need you to consistently encourage him, cheer him on, and continually support him, no matter how many mistakes he may make. You want to always convey to him that you have his back and you are willing and prepared to be good to him. When you do this there is nothing that the two of you cannot accomplish. In fact, the encouraging cheer of a woman is so strong, it helps motivate a man to accomplish things he never thought he could. Why do you think sport teams hire 'professional encouragers' called cheerleaders?

**WHY IS HE ALWAYS HANGING OUT WITH HIS BOYS?**

Jade and Rich had been seeing each other for some time. They seriously discussed marriage and their future goals. But, all of a sudden, they called things off. Jade told me that all Rich wanted to do was hang out with his buddies. I asked Jade, "When Rich tells you he is getting ready to go out, what do you do?" She answered, "I usually get upset with Rich, then we start arguing and, before you know it, he storms out the door and I run into the bedroom in tears." So, I asked Jade,

"What do you think would happen the next time Rich came to you and told you he was going to hang out with his boys, if you didn't react like you usually do, but responded by asking him if he would like you to go along? Or, if you weren't up to going, you told him to go ahead and have a great time?"

She countered, "Why would I say that? I don't want him to be hanging out till all hours of the night. Besides, it's not safe out there, and a mature adult wouldn't act the way he is acting." I replied, "This problem is not so much about how Rich is acting, but how you are re-acting. When you allow Rich or anyone, for that matter, to get you emotionally upset and cause you to react the way you do, you become a victim of your own emotions. Consequently, you end up saying and doing things you later regret." I continued, "Instead of letting your emotions get the best of you, you should get the best of them by putting them in check."

Usually, when a woman first gets into a relationship, she is willing to go anywhere and do almost anything, so she can enjoy her man's company. But, after a few years (and in some cases, months) into the relationship, she stops doing the things that made him fall in love with her to begin with.

She won't go to the gym with him. She won't go play, or watch him play, basketball. She won't go golfing or fishing with him. At first, even though she really didn't like to do those things and really thought those things were a little silly, she was willing to do whatever was necessary to be with him.

You must understand, because of a man's innate desire to compete, he is going to want to go play basketball, go golfing, or go fishing or just hang out with his boys. This gives him the opportunity to create an environment that makes him feel like he is winning. This is where we get the word 'recreation'. Every man wants to 're-create' a competitive environment that makes him feel like he is winning. He needs this time. And, if he can't enjoy this time with you, he is going to find someone else with whom he can enjoy it. In many cases, it is going to be with the guys. But in far too many cases, it's with a woman who is smart enough to know that if she is 'good' to him and shares in his recreational time, soon enough, he will want to return her goodness and share precious moments with her.

I have seen this happen on the basketball courts. There was a young girl who came to the basketball courts to watch her man play ball. At first, many of the older guys made comments about this girl keeping a watch on her man, so they laughed and snickered. But, soon it was evident they were jealous of this guy, because after seeing her at the basketball court a few times, some of the guys would say, "Man, I couldn't get my girl to come out here, not without me hearing about it later."

See, these guys wanted their ladies to be with them, but felt if their ladies did come out to the basketball courts, they would regret it later. They could just imagine the punishment coming. Either their ladies would fuss about them playing ball all day, or would expect repayment by requiring these guys to spend the rest of the week going shopping with them.

So, all this young guy's girl did was sit out there and cheer her boyfriend on. Now, how do you think that made him feel? Not only did it make him feel like a star, he started acting like one. His basketball skills got better and better. The more she encouraged and cheered him on the better his game got.

Now, I bet you this young lady didn't have to twist his arm to take her out on a date or go shopping with her. Because she was good to him and willingly gave to him what he needed, there is nothing he wouldn't do for her.

***To be a helper for the Man***

Because everything about a woman was designed by God to help the man to fulfill the vision that God put in his life, a woman is going to always want to be a part of what is going on in her man's life. And it is not so much she wants it, but she needs it. It's part of her makeup.

But helpers don't take over.

In Ephesians 5:22 it says, "Wives submit yourself unto your own husband, as unto the Lord." The word 'submit' has been greatly misused and abused over the years. The prefix sub means 'under'. The root word 'mit' comes from the word 'mission', which means purpose or vision in motion. So, a woman is made in such a way that she has no problem coming under or supporting a man who has purpose or a vision for his life. But, you can't submit to something or someone who isn't going anywhere or who doesn't want you involved in their mission. That is why, as a woman, before you get involved with a man, you must know his purpose or mission and decide if you want to be a part of it.

Not too long ago I heard a story about a rich man's wife who was having an affair with a struggling young artist. Some folks wonder how could this be? What need was this struggling artist supplying this woman that her rich husband wasn't able to supply. Her need to be 'needed'. The struggling artist didn't have anything but a dream. Yet, he made this woman feel like she was a part of his dream. The rich husband had already attained his dream and, at this point in his life, didn't think his wife needed to be concerned with what he was doing.

Don't get me wrong, though, this woman wasn't a total fool. She still wanted her rich husband's money, but also needed to have her <u>desire</u> to be 'needed', or to be a 'helper', fulfilled.

## WHY GOD PUT THE WOMB IN THE WOMAN

It was God who realized Adam needed a helper. In other words, God didn't just make the woman and tell her she must help the man. First, God decided what He wanted this being to be and do, and then He decided to make it. So, when God created the woman, He put in her the necessary components or wiring to be able to carry out the role of being a helper.

In order to carry out this role, God put inside this being, whom He was about to make, a womb. This womb has components built in so that whatever you give it, it receives it, develops or incubates it, multiplies it, and then gives it back to the giver. Case in point: If you give a woman a sperm, she will take it, incubate it, multiply it, and give it back to you in the form of a baby.

I had a young lady at one of my meetings tell me that she and her fiancé had been at a restaurant, talking about their future plans. He told her about the three-bedroom house he hoped to buy in his old neighborhood, and the next thing she knew, they were leaving the restaurant, mad at each other. So I asked her what she said in reply to his idea about the three-bedroom house. She said, "I thought he was limiting himself and we shouldn't move back to his old, rundown neighborhood, but should look for a newer and larger house in one of the new neighborhoods on the other side of town."

I suggested to her that what might have happened was that she took his little dream and expanded it, and this made him feel like his dream wasn't good enough. Even though it was most likely where he needed to go, she probably took him there too fast. In other words, she took his little dream seed, incubated and multiplied it, and gave it back to him in the form of a bigger dream. But, since most men don't understand this part of a woman, many men feel as though their woman "is putting too much pressure" on them or that you "just can't satisfy a woman!"

Jesus understood this about women. He knew, once a woman got some information, she would multiply it all over the world. That is why, when Jesus rose from the dead, He didn't show himself to the Apostles, Peter and John, first. Instead, He hid himself and waited until Mary got there. That was because he knew this receiver, Mary, was wired with a womb that would cause her to take the gospel all over the world and never stop talking about it. But the men would have done what they usually do when they don't see things happen the way they think they should. They forget. In fact, many of the disciples had already lost hope and forgot that Jesus promised them He would rise on the third day. That is why, when he finally showed up, they were afraid and thought they had seen a ghost.

**TO BE SUITABLE FOR THE MAN**

In Gen. 2:18 God says, "I will make a help meet for him". The word 'meet' here is an old English word that means 'fit' or 'suitable'. In other words, God is going to make this creature, called woman, so that she can 'fit' the man.

In Proverbs 12:4 Solomon says, "a virtuous woman is a crown to her husband…" Think about that for a second. First of all, who wears a crown? A king. And if a king is going to wear a crown he is going to choose a crown that 'fits' him and exudes his glory and honor. No king wants to wear a crown that is all tarnished and made out of fake jewels. Nor does a king want a crown that doesn't 'fit' him right. Because it would be easy for another king, or anyone else for that matter, to look at his crown and know something is wrong. In other words, the better looking, better fitting, and more expensive the crown is, the more respect the crown wearer, or the king, gets.

47

It also says in 1Cor.11 that the woman is the glory of the man. The word glory means expressed image or true nature. Just as Jesus is the glory or expressed image of God, so is the woman the expressed image of man. So, if you want to know what God is like, you can look at Jesus and, if you want to know what a man is like, you don't have to ask him. Just take a look at his crown (his wife) and you can figure him out.

# Chapter 4
## How A Man Interprets Love

Most women think all men want is sex. But that is not true. Sex is not a man's greatest need. A man's greatest need is honor and respect. That is how he interprets Love. For a man respect equals Love. Say it over and over again until it sinks in, for a man, "Respect equals Love."

Since we know the nature or innate characteristic of a man is to lead, we must understand that leaders run on respect. God never did command the woman to 'love' her husband. But you always hear God telling her to respect and honor him. In Eph 5:33, Paul says, "let the wife see that she reverence her husband." The word reverence, according to *The New Webster Dictionary,* means an attitude of deep respect and esteem, mingled with affection.

On talk shows, you see it time and time again. Here is this woman coming on this talk show to reveal to her boyfriend that she isn't really the woman he thought she was. In fact, she is not a woman at all… she is a man posing as a woman, or a transsexual. People always wonder, "How could this happen? How could this man not know that this transsexual wasn't a woman, since he's been dating her for the past six months?" But the poor guy says, "How was I supposed to know she wasn't a woman. She looks like a woman. She acts like a woman. And since we never had sex, I couldn't tell." What?! Never had sex! How could this guy go out with this woman for six months and never have sex with her. How? Because, it was giving him something greater than his need for sex, it was giving him respect.

> *Respect is something so necessary to a man's makeup, it motivates a man to do things for a woman that he never thought he would do.*

I know of this particular young couple that dated for three years. The young lady in this relationship believed that the reason she and her boyfriend weren't married yet was because they were waiting for the 'right time'. Baloney! Three months after we had this conversation, they broke up. Within six months after they broke up, he married another woman of a different race. I mention this because I know the guy. And I know he didn't just wake up one morning and say, "I am going to marry a woman of a different race". The race wasn't important to him. It was the way this woman made him feel. This new woman was making him feel that he was the best thing going, simply by giving him the respect he craved. He appreciated the way she treated him so much, he didn't want her to get away, so he married her.

How was she giving him respect?

She may have done something simple, like wearing her hair the way he liked it, or by wearing the clothes that he liked. Or, instead of embarrassing him in public, she laughed at his silly jokes, even when nobody else was laughing. Or, she does one of the best things a woman can do for a man. She does her best to keep a positive and happy attitude.

In essence, what I am saying is, all she did was find out what he needed and gave it to him. Sounds simple, doesn't it? Well, it is. First, you find out what the product needs, then you find a way to get it (the product) what it needs; in turn, the product will give you what you need.

I usually ask people if they have ever been fishing. If they have, I'll ask them what kind of bait do they use to fish with. Usually, they will say worms, crickets, etc. So I ask them if they eat worms? I usually get an emphatic, "No!" Then I'll say to them, "but the fish eat the worms, right?" See, they know if they want to catch fish, they don't want to give the fish what they want; they give the fish what the fish wants and in turn they get the fish. This simple truth works for your boss, co-worker, mother, father, sister, your vehicle, your dog, fish, etc.

See, respect for a man can be interpreted in different ways. We talked earlier about the receiver of love determining what love is. As a woman, you shouldn't just assume you know what your man wants, instead ask him. And don't assume what he wants from you today is what he is going to want from you tomorrow. One day, he may want you to wear that sexy red outfit when the two of you go out. The next day, he may want you to wear those tight jeans you have hidden in the back of your closet.

**WHAT IF HE WANTS ME DO SOMETHING I DON'T WANT TO DO?**

A lot of women believe, if they give their man what he needs, they are losing a part of themselves. They feel that, in order to give a man respect, it means doing things they don't want to do and disrespecting themselves. Nothing could be farther from the truth. The more you sow the right kind of seeds, the more you reap. But, I admit, in any type of relationship, there must be communication... with compromise. However, it is important for you to discern if your reason for not wanting to do what your man wants is based on a good foundation.

What do I mean by that? Let me give you an example. I have a client I'll refer to as Rita. Rita says her husband Bruce wants her to wear sexier outfits when they go out with some of his coworkers. Rita contends that the outfits Bruce wants her to wear are too sexy and too revealing. She says, as a mother of two, there are certain things she feels she shouldn't wear.

Before I came to any conclusions, I asked her to describe the outfit Bruce wanted her to wear. She did better than that. She showed me a picture of the outfit in a magazine. After looking at the outfit and looking at her, I asked Rita what was wrong with that outfit. In my opinion, the outfit didn't look like it would be too revealing or too sexy for her. I also told her, with her figure, the outfit would look better on her than on the model in the magazine.

So I asked her my favorite question, "Where did you get that from?" "Get what from?" Rita asked in return. I said, "Where did you get the idea that wearing an outfit like that is not appropriate for 'a mother of two'?"

After probing Rita a little further, it turned out that when she was a young teenager and her body began to develop, the older women in her family rebuked her for "wearing skimpy outfits to seduce the older men" around the neighborhood. Rita said she didn't understand their reasoning because she was too young to comprehend how her body was developing. She only knew that it was hot outside and, when it was hot, she always put on her favorite tank tops.

That memory of how she was treated scarred Rita so much so that it is controlling her today. That is why I said: in any relationship, there must be communication plus compromise. Communication will force Rita and Bruce to dig deep within themselves and deep within one another to search out their reasoning for not doing what the other one wants. Compromise will help Rita and Bruce to understand each other as Rita attempts to overcome her past. Right now, Bruce may not know why Rita doesn't want to wear the outfits that he likes. All he knows is, when he asks his wife to wear the outfit he likes, she says, "No". So he interprets Rita's unwillingness to do what he asks her to do as a lack of respect (love) from her.

To top things off, Bruce works in a professional environment, where the women dress to impress. And, when Bruce mentioned to one of his beautiful and sexy coworkers that she had a nice outfit on, not only did she wear the same outfit again the next week, she also bought some similar outfits and wore them every time she knew Bruce would be working with her group.

That is how so many affairs get started. Here is this other woman (or man) doing the things the spouse won't do – right down to wearing the 'too sexy of an outfit for his wife to wear'.

If we stop and ask ourselves where we get most of our prejudices or beliefs, we will soon discover that most of them are based on opinions from other people who are in bondage themselves and want us to be in bondage, too. And, since you have the right in Jesus Christ to be free, you should refuse to be in bondage to anyone or anything.

That is why, in this book, I discuss the spiritual side of things. Everything that goes on in our lives is first conceived in the spirit realm. So, it is imperative to not only look at the way things are in your life, but find out why they are the way they are. If you trace them back, you will realize everything stems from a spiritual root. Once you find that root, measure it up to what the Word of God says about it. If it doesn't measure up to the Word, don't toy around with it. Take your spiritual sword, which is the Word of God, and cut it to pieces.

Note: The prerequisite to that means that you must know what the Word of God says.

Now, hold up. I know what you are going to say. You are going to argue that if Bruce loved Rita, he would understand why Rita didn't want to wear the outfits he wanted her to wear. Now, it seems funny to me that, whenever I address this topic in my meetings, the women who use this argument are the same ones that have no problem dressing the way their employer expects them to dress; yet, have a hard time dressing the way their husband wants them to dress.

What does the Word of God have to say about this? The Word says in 1 Corinthians 11:9, "Neither was the man created for the woman, but the woman for the man." We just skip right over those few little words in the Bible. God was trying to let us know that He was not making this woman for her employer, or for her children, or for her parents, or for her pets. He made her for the man, period.

See, no matter how Rita determines to dress, her dress code is going to be influenced by some man. Why do I say this? Because Rita is basing her dressing on how she feels. She can allow her feelings to be determined by the older women in her past, who were no doubt influenced by the men in their lives, or she can allow herself to be influenced by what her boss thinks is 'appropriate'. Or, she can use wisdom and make sure she is pleasing *her* man first. Once her man knows she respects him in this way, this will no longer be an issue for him.

## GIVING HIM WHAT HE NEEDS VS. WHAT HE WANTS

A wise woman must be able to determine what her man needs versus what he wants. And then find a way to give it to him. For example, if you are not married to a man, but he wants sex from you, you have to determine what's more important. Giving him the sex he wants or giving him the respect that he needs, by you respecting yourself.

See, a man's (or a woman's) wants may change, but his needs never change. That is true in every aspect of life. For example, today you may be hungry so you need food to satisfy your hunger. But, to satisfy that need for food, you may want some fried chicken. Tomorrow, when you get hungry, you may not want fried chicken to satisfy your hunger. You may want a salad or a piece of fruit. Either way, you're going to need something to satisfy your hunger. The need is constant but the want is not.

To show a man you love him, he needs you to give him respect. Remember, for a man, respect equals love. Today his need for respect may be satisfied by his want, or rather desire, for sex. But, that could change by tomorrow or within the next hour. Tomorrow his need for love may be satisfied, simply by having you listen to his dreams or ideas, without saying anything negative about them.

The same holds true for a woman. A woman was created to be loved. But, to satisfy her need for love today, she may want to hear a kind word. Or, she may want her man to take her out to a nice quiet restaurant that evening. And, later on that night, she may just want to be held.

Get my point?

This is a powerful principle. Because, once you know and

understand a person's needs, you know that in a matter of time, you can get that person to do whatever you want, just by supplying their need.

## THE BABY COMES FIRST

I know many couples, whose relationship started to deteriorate, as soon as they had a baby. In fact, it started, in many cases, before the baby even arrived. That is because the man can sense that once the baby arrives, his needs will become secondary. And, many women feel that their newborn is priority. The baby does have needs. And, of course, your husband knows that. But, you must understand, if he feels he is not getting the respect and attention he deserves, he will begin to regret having the child.

A wise woman will give attention to the baby, but, because she understands the nature of men – and her man in particular – she will let him know in words and deeds that he is the most important thing in her life.

Now, I did not say you should abandon your baby for any man. That is not wisdom. That is foolishness to the "nth" degree.

Let me tell you a story. Of course, I know you have seen or heard of cases similar to the one I want to share with you. This lady I knew had a nice husband and twin girls. She had the girls late in life and her labor was very long and very painful. After the two girls were born, she was so happy to have them, she decided to be the best mom she could be. Her relationship with the girls grew very close, but her relationship with her husband grew distant. After a couple of years, he started having an affair with one of his co-workers. Then, after a few more years, they split up. As the girls grew, they started asking questions about the whereabouts of their daddy. Their mother tried to get them to understand, as best she could, why daddy left and why he wasn't coming back. These sweet little girls began to change. As the girls grew older, they became more and more disrespectful to their mother. In fact, they began to dislike their mom. One of the girls claimed she hated her mom.

The mother took the girls to a family therapist to seek help in dealing with them. The therapist asked the girls why they treated their mom so terribly, especially since their mom had done so much for them and loved them so much. The girls' reply was, "If she loved us so much, why did she leave our daddy?"

Can you imagine that? Here was a mom, trying to give her girls the world by showing them her love. However, what the girls wanted and needed was for mommy and daddy to stay together.

Now, we know the mom is not totally at fault here. For a relationship to break up, it takes two. But, since daddy was not around, the girls took their hurt and frustration out on the person they could see... their mom.

# Chapter 5

## How He Communicates Vs.
## How She Communicates

*"You can get a man to do anything you*
*want if you* listen *to him long enough"*
*– Author Unknown*

To a man, words spoken are perceived as information. To a woman, words spoken are an emotional experience. If you tell a man he is ugly, he will say that you are ugly too and keep moving.

If a man tells a woman she is ugly, those words go right down into her womb where she receives it, incubates it, multiplies it and then gives it back to him. Then, five years later when he tells her how beautiful she is, she says to him, "you didn't say that five years ago when you called me ugly". And the man says, "I never said you were ugly". And she says, "Oh yes you did!" And she proceeds to tell him when he said it, what he was wearing when he said it, the expression on his face when he said it, where they were sitting when he said it, the time of day when he said it, and the exact words he used to say it.

**HE IS LOGICAL. SHE IS EMOTIONAL.**

Why do men and women perceive words so differently? Because, when communicating, a man tends communicate more logically and a woman tends to communicate be more emotionally.

But, let me say this right now, before I go any further: one is not better than the other. Communicating logically is not better than communicating emotionally or vice versa. They are just different ways of communicating. Actually, effective communication involves both logic and emotion. Plus, men are not one hundred percent logical, and women are not one hundred percent emotional. They both have a mixture of logic and emotion.

The reason men tend to communicate more logically and women tend to communicate more emotionally is based on the roles they are destined to carry out. Because the man was created to be the head of the family and to lead his family, his community and, therefore, his nation, the way that God has directed him, the man is going to be more logical in his thinking. A leader cannot be led by his emotions.

Imagine having a husband, who you look to, to be the head of the house and your protector, but is led by his emotions. You come home with tears in your eyes to tell him the terrible news about getting laid off from your job and the terrible way in which they let you go, and, before you can finish telling your story, he bursts into tears.

Now, is that the kind of man you want? I didn't think so. Everyone, man or woman, wants someone who is going to take the time to understand them, not be like them.

That is why, in the previous story about Rita and Bruce, if Rita does want to effectively communicate to Bruce, she must understand that Bruce is going to communicate from a logical point of view. A logical person wants information. He wants to know the facts, the bottom line. Then, he wants to take that information and disseminate it in order to come up with a solution.

But, this is not what Rita wants or needs. What she wants is to be able to express her feelings without being judged or without him trying to rush through her talking to get to the solution. Once she is able to talk to Bruce about her past not only will her love for him increase, she may also come up with her own solutions or be more receptive to his.

You might reason that, if Bruce wants Rita's love to be greater towards him, he should be willing to let her express herself as she needs to. This is true. But, just like you can't expect a person who speaks German to be able to communicate to a person who speaks English, a woman shouldn't expect a man to know how to communicate to her and a man shouldn't expect a woman to know how to communicate to him.

This is why communication is such an important part of any relationship. Whether it is between a man and his wife, or between a man or woman and God, there must be communication.

**YOU DON'T FALL IN LOVE. YOU GROW IN LOVE.**

That is why love is a growing process. Not something you fall into. You should never expect to 'fall' in love. But you can expect to 'grow' in love through your communicating and sharing with one another.

If you were in Rita's place, instead of throwing your relationship to the wind and getting upset with the way your man is or starting to believe that he doesn't care, stop and realize that if you abort this relationship for a new one, you may find yourself in a similar situation, if not worse. That is because there are far too many men and women who don't understand how to communicate with the opposite sex, so it just might be better to work with the one you're with. But, since you are now one of the ones who have a better understanding of this, it is going to be up to you to share with others (not by what you say, but by what you do) how to communicate with the opposite sex.

### I'M A COMMUNICATOR. HE'S NOT.

I remember a couple of years ago my wife and I were having some 'intense fellowship' (in other words, we were arguing) over our financial situation, on our way home from a Wednesday night bible study. She was drastically concerned about how we were supposed to get some bills paid that were coming due the next week. As she talked, I continued to drive, listening and every so often throwing in a few "uh hums" and a few "yeah, that's right". But, the more she talked, the more upset she was getting and the quieter I became. After a while, I wasn't responding at all.

Then she said, "Don't you even care about our financial situation? Am I the only one in this relationship who is concerned?" Boy, that got me hot. I said, "Concerned? Of course I'm concerned! I go to work everyday and work my butt off! How can you say I'm not concerned?" She said, "Well, you don't act like it." I said, "Oh, I know what you mean. You mean that I must not be concerned, because I don't act the way you think I should be acting; or I am not acting the way you are acting."

I had to remind her that just the mere fact that I was there, and I was listening, said I cared. And, just because I didn't get emotionally and visually concerned like she did, didn't mean I wasn't as concerned as she was.

Many women feel like their man just doesn't like to communicate to them. This is because they believe that in order for him to be communicating to them, he has to communicate the way they think he should be communicating. They don't realize that, all the while, he has been communicating to her, but she hasn't been hearing him. When men communicate, they do it the way they are made up, logically. When women communicate, they do it the way they are made up, emotionally.

Since he is logical, he is going to be solution oriented. So, what he is trying to communicate to you must pass through his mind. In other words, he must think it through first. Now this may take some time, but if you don't understand this, his way of communicating becomes frustrating to you. Plus, you end up wanting him to communicate like you do. But this won't work.

If you are a talker, you want him to be a talker. So, since he isn't communicating to you like you think he should by talking to you, you write him off as being insensitive or uncaring. And you figure that, if he is so insensitive and uncaring to your needs, you are better off either by yourself or with someone else. And, because you did not invest the energy to get the right knowledge, you simply jump out of one relationship and into another, only to find yourself in the same predicament again.

**HOW DO I GET HIM TO TALK TO ME**

When trying to get him to communicate to you, don't ask your man about what he is feeling. Feeling is an emotion that does not compute with him. (Note: I did not say he doesn't have feelings.) He is trying to process what you are saying through his mind (his logical side), and you are trying to get him to talk through his feelings or his emotional side. When this happens, a man will most likely clam up, short circuit, and decide to not say anything. Which makes you even more irritated. Or, he will do like most men do, either he will get angry and walk away or get angry and attack.

It is imperative that you *do not* come to any conclusion until you find out what he is thinking.

*Marva says that she and her husband Pete just aren't made for each other. They don't see things eye-to-eye; they don't have an intimate relationship; and they don't even talk that much to each other anymore. Marva says that every time she wants to talk to Pete, he just clams up or walks away from her. She laments that all she wants is for him to talk things out with her. For her, it would show he cares. Pete says all Marva does is fuss and argue. He doesn't mind talking, but he hates arguing with her. And, if she would just give him a little space to get his head together, he wouldn't mind so much talking with her. But, she just won't back off. When she's ready to talk, she keeps insisting that we talk and that they talk now.*

If Marva wants Pete to talk to her, she is going to have to allow Pete room to think his thoughts through. A good way for her to do this is to ask Pete when he thinks it will be a good time for them to meet so they can talk. (Notice I said, when 'he thinks'. If a man feels like you are in control or pushing the idea on him, it will cause him to back away from the idea.)

Marva should set a time and date not too far in the future because, anything after a few days, most men will forget. And setting a time and date is important to a man, because it appeals to his logical side. Now, at first Pete may reject being cornered into setting a time and/or date, because he may still associate this 'meeting' with arguing and fussing and believe that she is still trying to control or dictate the situation. So

Marva should let Pete know up front that there will be certain boundaries in this meeting, which can't be crossed, such as, no yelling, no name calling, and no finger pointing. And, there will be no use of words like 'never' and 'always'. In other words, they wouldn't want to say things like, "You never listen to me" or "You always wait for me to pick up after you." Now, if Pete continues to put off this meeting, Marva should write down her concerns and ask Pete to read it over at a time convenient to him.

Do you see what is happening here? Since Marva is not being pushy, Pete does not feel threatened by Marva. And Marva is learning that by allowing Pete to feel like he is in control, and by her writing out her concerns and organizing her thoughts, she is learning different and better ways of communicating. Plus, by Marva keeping her emotions in check, she is not allowing how she feels about the situation to dictate how she acts.

See that is what this book is all about, you being in control of you. You can't control other people but you can control you. And the more you learn from your mistakes and do what it takes to be a better you, the wiser you become. And as your wisdom increases so does your value – to the point where you become priceless.

# Chapter 6
## Strong Woman/Weak Man

There are a many people who are of the opinion that women today are a lot stronger than men. Or, when talking about a particular couple going through a difficult time in their marriage, they will point out the woman as the stronger one in the relationship.

But don't be fooled into believing this lie. The whole purpose of this lie is to make women feel like they are smarter, stronger, and better than men, which promotes the 'I don't need a man' philosophy. But just as much as men need women, women also need men.

*Strength in God's eyes is not measured by what you do, but by your obedience to God's Word.*

But, let me explain to you why that cannot be, especially in a marriage relationship. For a woman or man to be strong in a relationship they must have a strong partner. In other words, no matter how strong you might think you are as a woman, if the man you are called to 'help' is weak or not functioning in his right position, it doesn't mean you are stronger. It simply means you are carrying more weight than God created you to carry. Which in turn makes you weaker.

To prove my point, let me ask you a question. Who is stronger, a man carrying two full buckets of water across a hundred feet of rocky terrain or a woman carrying four full buckets of water across a hundred feet of the same rocky terrain? (All things being equal.)

And let's say, the purpose of getting the buckets of water across a hundred feet of rocky terrain is to provide water to 12 young children, who are dying of thirst, and to minister to their needs. (I need to be graphic so that you can get the picture.)

At first glance at this question, your answer might be the woman, because she is carrying four full buckets of water and the man is carrying only two and she can therefore, supply more water to meet the needs of the thirsty children. But ask yourself, with all things being equal, how can a woman with two arms and two legs carry four full buckets of water across a rocky terrain? The answer is, she can't. She may reach her destination but, when she gets there, the buckets will not be full anymore and she will be worn out. Which means she won't have sufficient water for the thirsty children and she will be too tired to minister to their needs. So the purpose for carrying the water to the destination would not have been fulfilled.

So no matter how smart you are, how strong you are and/or how much education you have, if the purpose you were created to accomplish is not being fulfilled it magnifies your weakness not your strengths. So in a relationship, if you carry more weight than you were meant to carry, instead of making you stronger in the long run it will make you weaker.

**IF I DON'T DO IT, IT WON'T GET DONE**

Many women feel they have been forced into the position of carrying more weight and doing more than their share because their man doesn't step up to the plate to do what he needs to do.

You say you have to be strong because the man you married is nothing like you thought he would be. In fact, you may believe that all of the good leadership qualities he showed you before you got married, must have been just a good acting job because he doesn't do any of the things a 'real' man of God should do. Well, have no fear, there is help.

One of my clients was in this same type of situation. She was at the point of seriously walking out and leaving her husband. I asked her, "Why was she so ready to leave?" She quickly stated that, "He is too weak for me and I need a strong man." She went on to say that he didn't like her independent ways. She explained that before they got married, he admired her strong, independent ways. But now, her strong and independent ways have been a source of contention between them. They have been married for only six months.

The problem many women have with men is that they don't want a control freak, but they also don't want a wimp. But if you are married to a wimpy man or a 'momma's boy', what do you do? First of all, most women haven't seen what a real man is like, so they don't know what one looks like when he arrives. That is because, in many cases, they didn't see it in the first man in their lives, their father. Maybe they didn't have a father or, if they did, maybe their father didn't show them love from a Godly man. Or he probably let the wife run things.

Remember, I said if something does not function the way God intended it to, don't settle with the way it is. Chart it with the word of God. If it doesn't come up to par with the Word of God, cut it at its root by *speaking* and *doing* what the Word of God says concerning it.

Earlier in this book, I mentioned to you that in Proverbs 26:2b it says, "…so a curse (bad thing) causeless shall not come." This means if something bad is happening in your life, you played a significant part in it. But, it also means you have the potential to turn your situation around so that it works for your good. This is a good thing.

Why do I say that? Because once you know you have the power as a woman to influence your situations and, therefore, your life for the good, then you can 'respond' from a position of power instead of 'reacting' from the position of being a 'victim'.

So, if you're married to a weak man and nobody put a gun to your head to force you to marry him, there must be something in <u>you</u> that has to be dealt with first. It's not that you should go around blaming yourself. That won't get you anywhere. But, you must search within yourself to find out if you are doing all you know to do so that you don't encourage your man to act like a weakling or a momma's boy. And, if all you know to do still isn't working, ask God for more wisdom. The Word of God says in James 1:5 that "If any of you lack wisdom, let him ask of God who giveth liberally and upbraideth not and it (wisdom) shall be given to you."

**USING WISDOM TO DEAL WITH YOUR MAN**

You must use wisdom when dealing with your man because you may be promoting weakness in him without even realizing it. And this may have started way before you said, "I do."

For example, Let's say you two are in the car deciding on where you want to go eat. He asks you where would you like to go and you say you don't know. He says it doesn't matter to him because at this point he could eat anything right about now. (Note: Most men will say something like this just to end the conversation and get to the solution. In this case the solution is to get food in his belly.)

But you really don't know what you want so you press him to make a decision. He says, "I want to go to eat at that new steak restaurant down the street." But as soon as he decides where he wants to go you say that you don't want to go to a steak restaurant because, "It's too late for us to eat steak." And that, "We should eat something a little lighter." You continue, "Let's go to that new Sushi restaurant on 5th street."

Without realizing it you have done it again. You have encouraged weakness in him. You pressed him to make a decision and as soon as he made one you discredit it and decide to 'lead' him the way you want to go.

This is not using wisdom. The more you do this the more you discourage him from making decisions. And though your reasoning may be right about eating steak so late you must remember that men hate being wrong. And because men hate being wrong, when a similar situation arises and you ask him where does he want to go to get something to eat, he will more likely say something like, "It doesn't matter to me" or "wherever you want to go is fine with me".

But wisdom has a better course.

Wisdom would have said something like this. "Honey, that's sounds great. But I thought you said (your bringing back to remembrance his own words) we should stop eating heavy meals so late at night." (Now give him a way out, an opportunity to make another decision without feeling like his decision was a wrong (or bad) one.) "I wouldn't mind eating a salad or going to that new sushi restaurant down the street. But steak is also fine with me." Now don't say a word and let him decide.

Let's look at this from another point of view, the Word of God. The Word of God says, "...wives are to submit unto their own husbands as onto the Lord." The word 'submit' means to come under a mission or purpose. But if you are an independent woman and you have been taking care of yourself and paying your own bills for the past fifteen or more years, how are you going to submit to this man? How is this man going to tell you what to do, especially since he can barely take care of himself?

Well, even though you may be smarter than he is, make more money than he does, and get things done faster and better than he does, it still does not make you 'stronger' than him in the relationship.

Now granted, if the man is not a man at all (and by the way, according to 1Cor.11, a man is only a man when he is submitted to Christ), this may make things a little more difficult. But the last thing you want to do is usurp authority over him. The word 'usurp' means to seize and hold authority over by unlawful means. In other words, because of your knowledge, passed successes, education, etc. you decide that you will do things the way *you* thing they should be done because you *know how to do it*. And you use this leverage to justify your reasoning for being the final say or authority in your house. Or you may use things like sex, pouting, crying, reminding him of his passed mistakes, etc. as leverage to get him to give into you.

This is not how God intended it to be. In a marriage relationship, God expects you and your husband to sit down and come to an agreement on God's vision and direction for your family. But when it's all said and done, even if you do not totally agree on the direction that your husband wants to go, you still must give him support in your words and deeds. And encourage him to lead.

I understand that this may not happen overnight. But to help you muster up the faith to get to this point, remember what Romans 4:17b says, and start calling '…those things that be not as though they were'. In other words, start reminding him and yourself who he is in Christ. Do not base this on how you see him or what he is doing now. Instead, base it on what God says in His word about him.

Start quoting and saying things like:

> *"I am bone of your bone and flesh of your flesh and I have confidence in the God in you."*

> *"I trust your decision because you are more than a conquer in Christ."*

> *"God created me for you so wherever we go or whatever we go through I got your back."*

Boy that's going to blow him a way! It's going to make him start saying and doing things for you that you can only imagine.

> *When you function in your position, you cause other people to function in theirs.*

Not only do you want to "call those things that be as those they were" but you must try from now on, to resist the urge to burden yourself with every problem that arises. Every time he asks you, "What are we going to do about a particular situation?" turn to him and say, "I don't know honey; what do you think we should do?"

If you take the lead, (since you know how and what to do, because you have done it all your life), you're giving your man permission to be weak. Don't do it. Instead, take a step back and allow, or rather force, him to take his rightful position, which he will, if you do not say or do anything. Of course, you will want to help him come to the right decision by adding a few suggestions of your own. But, don't take over. Remember, helpers don't take over.

When he starts operating in his rightful role, he may make decisions that may not make sense to you. But at least he's trying. And the more practice he gets at making decisions, the better he will become.

You have to realize that most men have not been taught how to be a leader, especially in the home. So unfortunately, you will be the one who has to help him be that man that God intended him to be. But don't worry this will pay off significantly for you in the long run. Because God is not to be mocked, "for whatsoever a man soweth he shall also reap".

**OLD HABITS ARE HARD TO BREAK.**

Of course, my client in the previous scenario could do like she's done in the past and jump out of this relationship into another relationship. But if this happens, she will soon realize that the new relationship also has similar problems. That's because she has taken the problem with her. She hasn't taken the time to find out why every man she gets with turns out to be weak or a momma's boy. She hasn't taken the time to see her ways. Her frustration rises because she ends up attracting the type of person she really *says* she doesn't want. But her actions prove otherwise. And in reality she is getting just what she is putting out. Because she is trying to function out of her position and trying to be 'strong', she is actually being weak. Remember when you try to carry a weight that you weren't meant to carry, or function in a role you weren't meant to function in, instead of making you stronger it makes you weaker by magnifying your weakness. And since she is not functioning in her position, she will attract men that aren't functioning in their rightful positions.

Remember, when God puts you through training school, you don't get to go to the next level until you pass the final exam. In fact, if you fail, you have to repeat the course.

A few things that you should do to help your man get over that hump of going from wimp to man:

    ✓    Find ten positive things to say to him every day - even if you think it's not making an impact on him, still do this, because this is not just for him. It will help your attitude and increase your faith. Remember, we walk by faith not by sight.

    ✓    Ask him if he needs your help, every day - Erase any reason for him to believe you are fighting against him and not helping him by making yourself available to him every day. But, make sure you don't just assume you are doing what he needs you to do. Make sure you ask him. And remember, what he wants from you today may not be what he wants from you the next day.

    ✓    Talk to yourself every day to remind and define who you are in the Lord - Don't define yourself based on your past mistakes. Define yourself by what God says about you. And, according to God, you are the Head and not the tail, you are above and not beneath. You must say what God says about you out loud so your ears can hear it. And, you must say it with the confidence that God would say it, if he was standing in front of you.

✓ Pray for his increased success and wisdom, every day, at least three times a day - you can do this through out the day. You don't have to fall on your knees or go into your prayer closet. Just say a little prayer, while going about your daily activities that will reinforce your belief in what God says about him.

✓ Talk positive about him, even when he is not around - By talking positive about him, you are setting the atmosphere that makes him feel welcomed and appreciated, even when he is not in your immediate presence. And everyone, man or woman, girl or boy, wants to feel like they are welcomed and appreciated. Because, we all know how awful we feel when we come into a room when someone has been talking bad about us.

✓ Allow him to make mistakes - Whenever he makes a mistake, encourage him to get up and try again. And again. And again. Always make him feel you have faith in his ability to be a good leader.

### YOU ARE WHAT YOU EAT

Not only is it important that you speak the word over your man's life, but it is also important that you speak positive and uplifting words over your life. Earlier we talked about the fact that we are made up of two distinct parts, spirit and dirt. What you feed yourself determines which one of the two distinct parts will have the most influence in your life. Jesus said in Matthew 4:4 when tempted by satan that, "Man shall not live by bread alone..." Jesus was giving us a powerful message here. When you decide to eat today, you may eat fish, chicken, salad, broccoli, or whatever. But all these things come from the earth; therefore, they are made up of the earth's components, which is dirt or soil. So, it will satisfy your dirt house. But when you want to satisfy the spirit part of you, you must eat spiritual food. That is why Jesus goes on to tell satan in the rest of that verse, "...but by every word that proceeds out of the mouth of God."

In other words, we should eat the Word of God in order to nourish our spirit-being, who resides in our dirt house.

When your spirit being is malnourished, it becomes weak. When it becomes weak, your flesh or dirt house becomes stronger. And when the flesh is strong enough to overpower your spirit, lust is birthed. And lust is so strong, it will cause you to do and say things that you thought you would never do.

How many times have you said you were not going to do something and you did it anyway? Here you are trying your best to lose twenty pounds so you can fit into an outfit you want to wear to your high school reunion, but that chocolate candy keeps calling your name. It says, "Eat me. I won't harm you. I'm not going to add any more inches to your waist. I promise." So you eat it.

Or, how many times did you tell yourself that no matter what he says or how nice he is, "I won't sleep with him," only to find yourself in bed with him a few hours later– and mad at yourself.

This is because the desire of the flesh is to want things that are not edifying to the spirit. It's important that we eat the Word of God, our spiritual food, to keep us headed in the right direction.

# Chapter 7
## Preparing Yourself For Love

**S**ome of the things I see single women do are sincere. They really do put their heart into their actions. But, unfortunately, many of their actions *are sincerely wrong*.

### THE LOOK

I saw one of my clients out in the mall and she had this mean look on her face. I didn't say anything to her then, but waited till the next time she came to see me at my salon. I asked her about the day I saw her in the mall. I said, "I saw you in the mall last week and you didn't look too happy. Were you all right?" She said, "Yes. Why? Didn't I look alright?" I said, "No. You looked like you were mad at the world." She said, "A lot of times when I go out and don't want guys to approach me, I will put on my 'don't talk to me' face.

I asked, "Does it work for you?" And she said, "I guess it does."

Well, it just so happens I saw her out somewhere else and she had the same look on her face. But this time, I went up to her and spoke. I asked her, "Are you all right?" She said, "Why do you ask me that every time you see me?" I said, "Because you have that look on your face again. Do you not want any guy to try and talk to you while you are out here?" She said, "Yeah. I wouldn't mind." I said, "Well, how will a guy know whether you have your 'don't talk to me' face on or your 'do talk to me' face on'? She said, "If a guy wants to talk to me, he has to be brave enough to take that chance." I asked her my favorite question, "Where did you get that from? To me, it didn't make any sense. And, by the way, didn't you tell me you were tired of dealing with 'no good' men?" She said, "Yes". I said to her, "Don't you know the only kind of guy you are going to attract is the guy who, more than likely, has nothing going for himself. Why wouldn't he approach you? Nobody else is talking to you and he probably has nothing to lose."

**WEARING A WEDDING RING ON HER RING FINGER.**

Before I got married, I was involved with the singles ministry in our church. At one of our singles' fellowship, one young lady in our discussion group had a ring on her ring finger that looked like a wedding ring.

Now I knew she was single and currently not dating, but I wanted to get this out in the open so I asked her, "Are you engaged?"

She said, "No." I said, "Don't you want to get married someday soon."

She said, "I of course I do." I asked her, "Then why do you have a wedding ring on your ring finger?"

She said, "Because the Lord told me that I should be married to Him until He sends me the right man, and to wear this ring as a symbol of our marriage relationship." I asked her, "Are you sure it was the Lord? Because, if a good Godly man is interested in you and sees that ring, wouldn't he think you are already in a relationship with someone? And why would a good Godly man violate the marriage institution by trying to talk to a married woman."

She said, "If he is the one for me, the Lord would cause him to overlook the ring and approach me anyway." I said, "If he approached you anyway, after seeing you had a ring on, he may not be the type of man you want to get involved with."

Well, I wanted to make sure I wasn't the only guy in the meeting who was thinking this way. So I asked a couple of guys in the group what they thought. And sure enough, they were thinking the same thing I was thinking and glad I brought it up. But, because most of them didn't want to get the women in the meeting mad at them, they kept quiet.

Not me. I am the type of person who would want somebody to save me before I made a fool of myself. So, I try to treat people the way I want to be treated.

Needless to say, that ring idea didn't work for that young lady. In fact, years later when I did see her again, she was still wearing that ring and still single.

There are two things that concerned me about the above two incidents.

The first is that both women were sincere about what they were doing, but, unfortunately, they were sincerely wrong. They both wanted to meet a nice guy and to eventually get married, but they were both sending the wrong messages.

If you get an idea to do something, talk with someone that has some wisdom and understanding in that area. In fact, it would be wise to follow this spiritual rule, "Let every Word be established in the mouth of two or three witnesses". - Deut.19:15, Matt. 18:16, 2Cor. 13.1

And, the second thing is that they both have been doing these 'sincerely wrong' things for sometime, but nobody challenged them on it. This showed me that if a person is going in the wrong direction, the majority of people would let them continue going, even though they know they are headed off a cliff.

See, to a man, a stunt like that doesn't make sense. It doesn't fit into his frame of logic. In fact, because she is trying to build a Godly relationship on a false foundation, it won't come to pass. She will get a relationship all right, but it wouldn't be Godly.

I could see if the young lady who was wearing the ring wore it because she didn't want to be involved with anyone, besides Jesus or anyone in our singles fellowship. But, to wear the ring to get a man is ludicrous!

**THE RING – A SYMBOL OF LOVE...NOT!**

Now that we are on the subject, let's talk about the ring. I mentioned earlier that in the Bible days, when a man wanted to marry a woman, he had to bring a dowry, which is a valuable gift to symbolize his love or serious intent to marry a woman. Nowadays, when a man wants to show his desire to marry a woman, he gives her a ring.

Let me ask you a question. Is the ring primarily for her or is it primarily for him?

If you answered for him, you are right. Why? You see, a woman can stay with a man for ten years and not be legally married to him and still feel they have a 'committed' relationship. Not a man. A man will stay with a woman for ten years as long as he is getting what he wants from her. Then, after ten years, he can walk right out the door and leave her and the relationship behind and never look back.

I know of so many women who get caught up in the hope that 'someday when the time is right and we are both ready, my fiancé is going to pop the question.' And, in their minds, they can see themselves already at the altar, only to wake up some ten years later to the realization that they have wasted precious time and energy waiting on a lost cause and unfulfilled promises.

Let me encourage you to do your future husband, and yourself, a favor. Don't start making plans, or seeing the two of you at the altar, until you see a symbol of his love. The ring.

And, by all means, don't give your body to him- in other words don't have sex (any kind of sex) with him, until you have a ring from him (a symbol of his commitment), and you two have officially entered into the marriage covenant. You must have both.

If there is no symbol of his love and no covenant with you, and you have sex with him, he will not see you the same way he would have if you two had waited. And, I am not going to go into the problems that this sin brings into play. That is a whole other ball game.

Listen to me. He is not going to feel like you do. No matter how much he says he loves you or how much he says his feelings for you won't change, they will. His thinking will go something like this. He will think, first of all, that you must not value yourself very much if you gave yourself away so easily. And, who wants something that is not valuable?

Second of all, he will think that if you fell for him and his 'lines' so easily, what will stop you from falling just as easily for some other guy who has better lines than he has?

I know you are thinking: I have a commitment to him, I love him, I made all these plans for us.

Remember, he is logical, so his relationship with you has to make sense to him. And, although he loves you, his conclusion won't be based on his feelings for you or your feelings for him. Nor will it be based on the hype and the drama of being in a relationship. For him, all that will fade away. When it's all said and done, the only thing he will remember is that he got the prize, without paying the cost. And, for a man, this may cause him to come to the conclusion that this relationship doesn't make sense.

Hear what I did not say. I did not say for you to stop being nice to him. I did not say for you to stop doing the things that make you attractive to him. You don't have to dress differently. You don't have to wear long gowns every time you are around him. Allow him to continue to recognize your beauty. But also let him know that, "If he wants a bite of this fruit, he is going to have to let you know how much he values it." In other words, put up or shut up.

**WORDS CAN WEAR YOU DOWN**

Recently I was talking with one of my clients and she told me that she and her boyfriend just broke up. They had dated for over five years. Then, she went on to say this is third time in their five-year relationship that they have broken up. I said, "You guys looked pretty happy when I saw you two at the restaurant a few days ago." She said, "The only reason he took me out that day is because he was trying to get me back."

She went on to tell me that the reason they broke up in the first place was due to her finding out that he was sleeping with her best friend. So I asked her, "Are you going to get back with him?" She said emphatically "No!" Then sighed and said, " I don't want to, but, he is really wearing me down."

What she really was saying is that even though he was a liar and a cheat and he wasn't any good for her, his words were causing her to develop feelings for him again. See, now that he realized she was moving on with her life and the fling he had with her best friend wasn't working out, he figured he'd better get her back before someone else got her. So, he was taking her out on dates, telling her how much he loved her, treating her with tenderness, buying her nice things, etc. And, all these things he was doing, along with his tender, sweet, and romantic words, were slowly wearing her down. By telling her how much he has changed and how he much he loves her and can't live without her and that she is the apple of his eyes, and so and so on, and slowly, she started to give in.

And, though he wasn't ready before, now he was the one pushing her to marry him as soon as possible.

You must remember that, for a woman, words spoken are an emotional experience. So, even though that rascal wasn't planning on keeping his word, all the nice things he was telling her and doing for her made her feel like he is sincere and, just maybe, this time things will work out.

If she doesn't cut off all communication with him, she will find herself right back in a relationship that will eventually bankrupt her emotionally and kill her spiritually.

She should at least cut off all communication with him for no less than thirty days. This way, she will have time to see if he really is sincere about wanting to get back with her. And, she will be able to think clearly without being forced into making a decision that she will have to pay for the rest of her life.

If this guy is not willing to give her at least thirty days to get her thoughts straight and get his flesh under control, he is not serious about making a change.

## I'VE BEEN THERE

I remember, when I was in college, I met this beautiful young lady. She looked like she just stepped out of heaven. Boy, was she something! I really wanted to meet her. I would do all kinds of stuff to make sure that wherever she was going, I would be there. After finally meeting her, I found out she was just as nice on the inside, as she was beautiful on the outside. It turned out she was a nice Christian girl.

The more we saw of each other, the closer we became. She would even tell me stuff about the bible. (I didn't know much about the bible at this time.) And I would listen, too. In fact, I did whatever it took to be around her. I started thinking about us getting married, about us having children together. And I thought about where we would live and how we would be in love forever.

The more I was around her, the more I fantasized about us quenching our flames of passion. There was a part of me that felt like she was too precious to touch, in that way. But, there was also this other part of me that crushed that feeling and was willing to do whatever was necessary to get her in bed with me.

For about three weeks, she kept me at bay. (In college time that's like six months.) Then one day, when she felt like the time was right and that I had proved to her that I really loved her, by my constant begging and the fact that I was always around her, we made love. Actually, we had sex. And boy, was it good. As soon as I 'released' myself, my feelings for her changed.

I didn't even know why. I knew I loved her. Or, at least I thought I did. And I knew she was in love with me. And, of course, we waited until the moment was right, didn't we?

But what happened? Why couldn't I get myself to feel about her and see her in the same way?

Well, after that, needless to say, our relationship went downhill. I became uninterested. I even noticed she was willing to have sex with me just to keep me coming around.

It was years later before I realized what had happened to me. I realized that there was no symbol or sense of commitment from me to her. She gave me her most precious gift and I didn't give her anything in return that could compare to it. Once I got what I wanted, I was off to find another challenge.

Some people may say I really didn't love her in the first place. I would beg to differ. The problem was not a lack of love. It was a lack of commitment. I had nothing I could look at to remind me of the price I paid to get her. To say to me, "Hey, Gil you did it, you won the prize!" I needed something to make me feel like I had invested something of value in this relationship.

I even remember treating her differently. I didn't do and say the nice things that I used to. That is because, in looking back, I realized I was mad at her. I was mad at her for giving into my constant begging for sex. Didn't she know that, as a man, this was what I was supposed to do? How could <u>she</u> have let this happen?

Didn't she know that, for me and for most men, all our lives, we are told to, "Sow your wild oats"? I was only doing what I was conditioned to do. But she, she was a Christian. She should've known better. She should have had better control over herself.

It's funny that, as soon as things don't work out our way because of our own dumb decisions, we look to blame other people for our mistakes.

I didn't know or understand that she was doing what she felt was right. To be honest, I didn't even care. I didn't understand or know that having sex with me was her way of giving me her most prized gift, and her way of showing me how much she loved me. All I know is, when I began to mull over our relationship in my mind, in my logic, for me it didn't make sense.

Later, when I finally did meet my wife and I came into the knowledge of who I was, and what God had planned for my life, I refused to give in to the temptation to have sex before marriage. I knew me. And I knew if I fell into temptation, I wouldn't be able to say years later that I paid the price in full for my wife.

# Chapter 8
## Selfish Lovers

Actually, the term 'selfish lover' is an oxymoron. Webster defines oxymoron as a figure of speech that places two contradicting words side by side.

You cannot really be in love with someone when your only thought is, "What can I get from this relationship?" And selfish people only think about what they want and need now. They are not concerned with how their selfish ways will affect them and others in the future.

In other words, your boyfriend says he really wants to and needs to 'make love to' (have sex with) you. Now, that rascal isn't thinking about anything but satisfying his needs. He is not concerned about fulfilling your needs. He is not concerned that you may feel that having sex will, in some way, solidify your relationship. He is not concerned that you might get pregnant, have a child, put your future on hold, and have to work two or three jobs to 'make ends meet'. He is not concerned that having premarital sex will put into motion a generational curse that will pass on to his child and to his child's child. According to Exodus 34: 7, where God says that He will, "Visit the iniquity of the fathers upon the children, and upon the children's children, unto the third and to the fourth generation. And now this unborn child will have to deal with strikes against him or her for something he or she didn't have any control over. In fact, nothing is important to him, other than what he wants at this very moment.

Now let me ask you something. Do you think that's love?

There are so many people who go into a relationship looking for what the other person can give to them and do for them. They never take the time to ask themselves if what they are willing to bring to the relationship is comparable to what they expect the other person to bring to the relationship.

I had a nice, young Christian lady tell me the guy she was seeing wasn't any good for her. I asked her why, and she said he didn't have 'enough going on' to be with her. I asked her what she meant by him not having 'enough going on'. And her explanation to me, which was based on information she was getting from her girlfriends, her momma, her co-workers, and her girlie books, was that this guy, "had to be making a certain amount of money, driving a certain kind of car, and living in the right area."

I told her I thought that was great and she should expect the best. If it's out there, why shouldn't she have it? My only question to her, though, was if he has to have all that going for him, what was she going to bring to the table equally as valuable? She said, "I have a great paying job." I said, "But what if you get pregnant? You told me you wanted at least three children and you wanted to be a stay-at-home mom for your kids because your mom was never around for you. So, if and when you get pregnant, you won't have your great paying job anymore."

She said he also had to be nice looking. I asked her what she was going to do about her looks. She told me she was not bad looking. I agreed, but reminded her of the 40 pounds she had said she needed to lose. She remembered, but also thought if he didn't like what he was seeing, then he definitely was not the one God had chosen for her. (I think it's funny how people throw God into a situation only when they can *use* Him to serve their best interest). I said, "Wait a minute. You're trying to tell me that it is all right for you to have certain standards to measure your potential mate by, but, it is not all right for your potential mates to have certain standards to measure you by."

She said, "A man should want to provide for his family." I said, "I agree that a man should provide for his family. But no man wants to provide for a woman who puts a list of demands on him, especially if, from his point of view, she is not putting any demands on herself."

When dealing with the opposite sex, what we sometimes fail to realize is that what is important to us may not necessarily be important to the other person. As in the situation above, the young lady put high importance on her great paying job. This is the main 'bargaining chip' she is using to get the type of man she wants. But, not all men put such high importance on a woman having a great paying job. Especially when he knows her job is going to get more attention and respect from her than he will.

Remember, it's the receiver who determines what love is, not the giver.

But the worst part is, this young lady is placing high value on a temporal and very superficial thing. Her job. She is sowing the type of seed that will attract this type of man. A man who places high value on temporal and superficial things. A man whose 'love' for her will be based on the seed or bargaining chip she used to get him, in this case, her great job. And as soon as she loses her superficially based bargaining chip, she will lose his superficially based 'love'.

Love based on the wrong foundation won't last.

## IT DOESN'T TAKE ALL THAT

That being said, I do think it's important to do what you need to do so that you can attract the type of man that you want in your life. Which brings me to a story about a friend of mine.

Before I met my wife, I had a good female hanging partner named Latonya. Latonya was always crying to me about getting older and not being married yet. She had told me on many occasions that she just couldn't find the right man. And I have to say, based on the guys I had the opportunity to meet that this was true.

One day, as we were riding in her car back to my house, she started complaining again about another attempt at a failed relationship. We were headed down a major highway. She was driving, talking, and flapping her hands, all at the same time, passionately telling her side of why this last relationship didn't work. When she paused to catch her breath, I quickly squeezed in a comment. I said, "Latonya, you could be married in less than a year, if you really wanted to." She jokingly responded, "Oh yeah, what am I going to do, have my father lead a man down the alter with his shotgun?" I gave her the 'I'm not joking' look to let her know I was serious. So she asked, "What am I supposed to do? I've tried everything." I said, "No you haven't." She said, "What? What haven't I done?" Now, at this point, several things were going through my mind. I had wanted, for quite some time, to suggest to Latonya some things I thought she might want to try and do. And, in the past, I would throw out hints, but she blew them off as if I was just joking. So this time, I really wanted her to either take what I had to say seriously or stop complaining to me about her unfulfilled love life. I said, "Latonya, I think you should concentrate on getting back into shape." Latonya took her eyes off the road and fixed them on me, for what seemed like a good two minutes, and then burst into tears. She said, "That's not it! A lot of guys don't even care about stuff like that; that's just your problem." Boy, why did I have to go and open my big mouth. I said, "Hold up, Latonya. I'm not trying to get you upset. Let me explain what I mean. You are right. A lot of guys don't care about weight or whether their ladies are out of shape because, in many cases, the guys are out of shape and overweight themselves." I continued, "You being in shape is not an 'issue' for the men you are trying to date, it's an 'issue' for you."

*"By your words shall you be justified, and by your words shall you be condemned"- Matt.12:37*

You see, it was Latonya who would always make an issue out of her weight. And, it was Latonya who complained that she needed to get back into shape. She was always making remarks of how she knew she shouldn't eat certain things because it went against her core beliefs. And, it was Latonya who prided herself on how she used to look. And, because she felt uncomfortable on the inside, with her current weight and shape, she unknowingly transferred that same feeling to the outside, especially to the men she came in contact with.

Let me explain it another way.

Let's say you one of your girlfriends has recently undergone cosmetic surgery for a nose job. And you know your girlfriend felt like they had an ugly nose all her life. So whenever she was around people for the first time, she always felt like people were staring at her nose. She also remembers how, all through her childhood years, the kids at school and some insensitive grownups would make negative comments about her unattractive nose. And even though she is now an adult and the cosmetic surgery has given her a new and attractive nose, the hurts of her past still haunt her. She still feels that whenever she meets someone new that they must be staring at her nose and she is sure that they are getting ready to make some kind of negative comment.

But that's not the case at all. People are just amazed at her attractive features and can't help but stare. And, of course, they don't want to be so bold as to ask her whether or not she has received cosmetic surgery.

Now back to my point.

Because this person hasn't dealt with the hurts of her past, she is still uncomfortable when getting stares from people she has just met. She even goes to the extreme of holding her head down so she won't give people the opportunity to say something negative about her nose. But as you can see, the 'issue' is not with everyone else; the 'issue' is within her. The insecurity that she is feeling on the inside is manifesting itself on the outside.

After several weeks had passed and Latonya started speaking to me again, she reminded me about what I said to her and how she still didn't like it, but when she went to the Lord about it in prayer, the Lord revealed to her that what I had said to her was true.

Well, eventually, Latonya did lose the weight and got back in shape. And, as she did, her attitude became more positive. And, as her attitude got better, she started dressing and looking better.

A few more months passed and I hadn't heard from Latonya. So, I decided to call her. When I reached her, she could barely contain the excitement in her voice. She said, "Gil, I hate to say it, but you were right. Since I got back in shape and started taking care of myself, I have met some great guys. Some of them, whom I have worked with for years, never even looked at me twice before now."

In fact, Latonya's newfound attitude caused even her female coworkers to try and 'hook' her up with guys they knew.

What was it? Was being out of shape the real issue for Latonya? No. I don't believe that was it at all. I believe it was the negative perception she had about herself that caused her relationship problems.

*When you don't feel or think good about*
*yourself you* can't *maximize your true potential.*

Now, I'm not saying every woman should go out and try to run fifty miles a day and become a 'thin mint'. Being overweight, or out of shape, may not be your 'issue'. Besides, your man may like you just the way you are. What I am saying is, you have to be woman enough to look at yourself, not in a critical way, but in the way God looks at you, and deal with your 'issue'. In other words, turn around and face your mountain. Believe me, it isn't that big. And determine to deal with it. Once you determine to deal with your mountain, you will realize it just seemed big, because you were looking at it from your point of view and not God's point of view. And, once you deal with your mountain, your inner beauty and outer beauty, can begin to shine, just like God intended.

# Chapter 9
## God Forgave You, So Forgive Yourself

There is a grievous crime being committed in our society today. And, the bad thing about this crime is that it is self-inflicted. This crime is not just against women only. It affects men, boys, and girls of all ages. Its name is abortion. But, the kind of abortion I am talking about is vicious, because this kind of abortion attacks the mind, body, and spirit of its victim. It takes its victims and kills their life force by killing their dreams, their aspirations, and their goals. And then, it leaves them limp and lifeless, like the walking dead.

There are a lot of women who seriously desire to have a meaningful relationship with a man but can't get past the hurt that has been inflicted upon them, either by what their fathers said and did to them or by what some other man in their life has done to them. And so, they turn on themselves. They end up believing that it's not possible to have a loving and meaningful relationship. And, if it is possible, they feel that it's not possible for them.

The only way you can truly have meaningful relationships is to forgive the person or persons who have done you wrong.

In the previous story about Latonya, I didn't tell you the reason she gained so much weight and got out of shape. It was because Latonya used to be married to a verbally abusive husband. His verbal abuse had Latonya seeing herself less than she was. So, before she could even deal with her weight 'issue', she had to deal with the abuse issue. And then, she had to forgive her ex-husband.

When you don't forgive someone of the sin or sins that they have committed against you, that very sin will enslave you. If you had a father who said you were "no good" and you wouldn't "amount to anything", as much as you hate what he said about you, you end up being "no good" and not "amounting to anything." If you had a parent who molested you, that parent may have gone to their grave, but you're still left carrying the burden of the unforgiven sin. The Word of God says for us to "lay aside every weight, and the sin which doth so easily beset us..."-Heb. 12:1b. I heard a minister say this scripture was in reference to the days when merchant ships had slaves aboard them. Many times, there would be fights and one slave would end up killing another slave. So the officers on board would have the dead slave's body chained to the man who killed him and cast them both into the sea. And, as you can probably surmise, the weight of the dead slave would soon drown the other slave, whom he was chained to.

It's the same way when we don't forgive someone of his or her sins against us. The dead weight we are carrying weighs us down. Then it begins to rot and stink. And, because it's a part of us, we begin to stink and to sink, too, because of the sins that we keep chained to us.

So before you can expect to have a true and meaningful relationship with a man or anyone, you must open up your heart and examine it for any spots of unforgiveness. And please, because it happened so long ago and you barely remember it, don't act like it's not affecting you now. As human beings, we have a way of putting things in the closets of our minds, hoping if we keep the door closed, the boogey man of past sins and hurts won't come out and get us.

But once you forgive that person or persons, don't stop there. Go to that person, if they are still alive, and tell them you forgive them. Tell them you have released them from anything they may have been responsible for doing to you, or allowing to be done to you, in the past.

And, if they are not willing to listen to you, or if they are no longer around, tell them you forgive them out loud, so your ears can hear it and your heart can begin to heal. And, once you confess forgiveness for them with your mouth, and believe it in your heart, then that settles it. Let it and them go!

This process is not going to be easy. And by all means, you getting to the point of forgiving this person may not happen overnight. But as you grow in the understanding of God's love and His forgiveness, you too will learn how to forgive and how to become free.

## ENCOURAGE YOURSELF

You are the most beautiful and precious creation God made. The scripture says, "the rib which the Lord God had taken from the man, made He a woman..." The word "made" here is not the same word God used when He made the man. The word "made" is the Hebrew word that means 'to build up or to construct' as a sculptor would do. In other words, when God decided to make the woman, He took His time and was very delicate with her because He wanted to construct her and build her so that she exuded beauty. He was like a master sculptor meticulously creating a masterpiece. With the man, He was more like a construction worker. He just gathered some mud and put him together.

That is why every woman is so precious in God's sight. The scripture says in 1 Peter 3:7 that, "husbands are to dwell with their wives according to knowledge giving honor unto the wife, as unto the weaker vessel." The word weaker means precious, valuable, and costly. It's not referring to weakness as in strength.

Because you are so precious in God's eyes, you can't allow anyone to treat you less than the way God sees you.

If a man is not willing to treat you like the precious being that God created you to be, he is not the man for you. And, now that you have more wisdom on how to 'deal wisely' with men, your value is even greater. So, if he wants you, he is going to have to come up to par with you. Don't dare come down to his level and decide to settle for any ole' man, just so you can tell the world you have one.

There is an important reason for you to remind yourself of how beautiful and precious you are in God's eyes. When you have been in an ungodly relationship, the negative effects of that relationship can weigh you down. So much so that, when you look at yourself in the mirror, you don't like what you see.

I dated a girl like that for a very brief time. All her friends said she was a 'nice' girl but just couldn't seem to find any nice guys. When I met her for the first time, I thought she was very attractive and very nice. But, the closer I tried to get to her, the more she pushed me away.

How? Every time I would tell her how pretty she was, she would say, "No I am not." And, every time I would tell her I wanted us to have a more serious relationship she would say, "No you don't. You don't want to date someone like me." I tried to convince her that I was serious about getting serious with her. But the more I tried to tell her I liked her and I wanted us to start dating more seriously, the more she tried to convince me that I didn't want that.

Well, after a while, I started thinking to myself that maybe there was something about her that I wasn't seeing. She kept trying to convince me that she wasn't the kind of young lady that I wanted to be with. And, because she believed she wasn't good enough to be with me, I started to believe it, too. And, as you probably concluded, that relationship didn't last very long.

That is why it is very important that you value yourself, first. Because how you see yourself is going to determine how other people see you.

Here is what I want you to do. Every morning when you wake up and every evening before you go to bed say this out loud:

*"I am a beautiful, attractive, kind, considerate,*
*goal-oriented woman of God. I was created to*
*be loved and to be respected. I choose to give love,*
*respect others, and respect myself. I take responsibility*
*for my actions. I am not led by my emotions but instead*
*I am 'led by the Spirit of God'. I can do and be*
*whatever I set my mind to, because God says I*
*can. And, since God said it, that settles it."*

This is so important because, unless you talk to yourself and believe you are someone unique and special, you can't convince anyone else.

# About the Author

Gil Bryan is a perfect example of how one can beat the odds and win at life. He endured the sudden death of his father when he was six, the loss of his brother in a head-on collision with a drunk driver in his third year of college, and the uncertainty of survival during his own military service in the Gulf War (Desert Storm). With faith and determination, Gil overcame these obstacles and rebuilt his life as a successful entrepreneur, coach and motivational speaker.

Gil's teaching of the differences between the sexes developed in an unconventional way. As an owner/stylist of a beauty salon and over 16 years in the beauty industry, Gil had the unique opportunity to interact with people on both a personal and professional level. The adversity he had faced in his own life and the spiritual peace he subsequently achieved fueled his desire to reach out and guide others who were experiencing emotional pain or turmoil.

In addition to being a successful businessperson for almost 20 years, Gil is a highly respected consultant, mentor, and educator. He has spoken to a variety of audiences, including youth groups, university students, employees, church organizations, and business leaders, on a wide range of topics, such as gender relationships, cultural diversity, self-esteem, leadership, and entrepreneurial development.

Gil currently resides in Covington, Georgia with his beautiful wife, whom he has been married to for over eleven years.

LaVergne, TN USA
25 September 2009
159065LV00001B/53/A